First Lessons®

Folk Banjo

by Dan Levenson

Online Audio www.melbay.com/22257BCDEB

Audio Contents

1	Tuning notes - Key of G	20	Basic strum with chords - Example 10, Line 1
2	First strum - Example 2	21	Basic strum with chords - Example 10, Line 2
3	Row, Row, Row Your Boat–I	22	Basic strum with chords - Example 10, Line 3
4	Chords in G - Example 3	23	Black Eyed Suzie
5	Chord exercise - Example 4, Line 1	24	She'll Be Comin' 'Round the Mountain
6	Chord exercise - Example 4, Line 2	25	Mountain Dew
7	Chord exercise - Example 4, Line 3	26	G scale - Example 11
8	Chord exercise - Example 4, Line 4	27	Free Little Bird
9	Chord exercise - Example 4, Line 5/6	28	Key of C - F chord - Example 12, Song pattern only
10	Row, Row, Row Your Boat–II	29	Froggy Went A'Courtin'
11	Basic stroke - Example 5 - Brush thumb quarter notes	30	Oh, My Darling Clementine
12	Basic stroke - Example 6 - Brush thumb eighth notes	31	Down in The Valley
13	Basic stroke chord exersize - Example 7, Last line only	32	Old Joe Clark–I - Capoed - Key of A
14	Row, Row, Row Your Boat–III	33	Old Joe Clark–II - VII chord
15	Little Brown Jug	34	Hammer–ons - Example 13
16	Cripple Creek–I	35	Pull–offs - Example 14
17	Sourwood Mountain	36	Slides - Example 15
18	Individual strings - Example 8, Last line only	37	Cripple Creek–II
19	Basic strum - Example 9		

MEL BAY®

WWW.MELBAY.COM

Acknowledgments

To my parents – long past – hosts of many *Hoots,* who taught and encouraged me
to sing and play music from an early age.

To my boys, Jon and Josh who put up with their daddy's music and even learned to play some of it!

I am likewise thankful for all of you who believe in and support old time music, and have given me the opportunity to make it such a large part of my life as we share it together with the world.

To Bruce Blackburn – A banjo playing friend, hiking companion and fellow traveler who has found it fitting to land in Yuma, Arizona and graciously offered to be a *Folk Banjo* test pilot.

Last but not least–
Thanks to Pete Seeger himself who started so many of us down the banjo path. I am glad to have heard and met him both as a child and as an adult. No amount of thanks can express my gratitude for his music, his dedication to the banjo and folk music. His very existance defines the style.

Dan is endorsed by and endorses the following companies
It is through their work and support that I am able to continue bringing you this music.
Mel Bay Publications, Banjo Newsletter, Eastman Banjos,
Gold Tone Banjos, John Bowlin Banjos, Lee Banjos, OME Banjos, Vega/Deering Banjos,
Elixir Strings, Clifford Hardesty Fiddles, Elon Howe Fiddles, Red Diamond Mandolins,
Audio–Technica, The Stewart MacDonald Co. and Taylor Guitars.

Tablature has been set with *finale*® *2012* software.

All sound tracks have been recorded with an Audio-Technica 2020 USB microphone
with a Bernunzio Music/Eastman Whyte Laydie style banjo
with Audacity® software which is copyright ©1999-2008 Audacity Team.
Web site: http://audacity.sourceforge.net/
It is free software distributed under the terms of the GNU General Public License.
The name Audacity® is a registered trademark of Dominic Mazzoni

Table of Contents

Introduction – Folk it! Starting at the beginning

Many people take exception to the term *Folk* music, as they all remember the great folk scare of the 1950s and 60s. Musicians such as Pete Seeger, Woody Guthrie and groups such as The Weavers, The Kingston Trio, The Limelighters and Peter, Paul and Mary were traveling the country singing Folk songs. They also did performances and hoots, or hootenannies, the folk equivalent of the jam sessions we know today. Here, the songs were king. Folk music became synonymous with folk songs where the banjo played the role of an accompaniment instrument, somewhat like the guitar playing chords and patterns to back up the singer – whose voice became the lead instrument. Pete was more of a singer who used a banjo to back up his singing instead of the other way around.

The folk style banjo is a different skill from what most old time banjo players are playing today. In today's old time music world, the banjo is a co-lead with the fiddler and plays mostly fiddle tunes. And, though many of the older folks tell us that most, if not all, of these fiddle tunes once had words, the tune is the point and few complete songs are sung. The musicians in that style tend to get into one key and stay there, playing tune after tune after tune for quite a while. It is a wonderful style, and if you want to learn that type of old time playing I would direct you to my book *Clawhammer Banjo From Scratch* (MB20190M) and the related DVD (MB5005DVD) or *First Lessons Clawhammer Banjo* (MB22258M) which will give you a good foundation in that style.

Now that you know the basic differences between styles, let's get you started on *Folk Style* banjo playing so you can sing yourself to fame on songs you know, and keep up with others on ones you don't (yet).

The Banjo is sometimes called America's instrument. I like to call it a USA or United States Amalgamation because it has such an old and varied past, ending up today as kind of a melting pot of peoples and their cultures. The banjo is a member of the lute family, which traces its roots to Assyria - a country that no longer exists. Its ancestors (roots) come to us from many places - most notably Asia (China's sanxian, a skin headed banjo type instrument, is said to date back over 4000 years), Africa and even Eastern Europe. If you want to see a vast representation of these instruments, I urge you to take a trip to the Musical Instrument Museum in Phoenix, AZ. It is a wonderful eye opening experience for this instrument and many others in our culture, along with virtually every other culture in the world and its music.

Today, you can find all kinds of banjo things with 4, 5, 6 or even 8 or more strings on them. For this book and style, we are going to concentrate on the 5–string banjo. It matters little whether you have a resonator (a wooden or metal cover on the back of the banjo) or not, as the only difference is that the resonator makes it a bit louder and heavier. Open back banjos tend to have a more mellow sound than the others. I prefer an open back instrument, but you get to choose. Just make sure it is a 5–string.

A NOTE ABOUT LONG NECK BANJOS - Pete Seeger is credited with the development of the *Long Neck* banjo, which is three frets longer than our standard instrument today, so he could tune to the key of E. Unless *you* sing in the key of E as he did, I would recommend against it as a first banjo. It just adds weight, and you will have to capo-up right from the start to be in G and play with other musicians. If you have one already, that's fine. Just be aware you will have to capo at the third fret for this book.

Parts of your banjo

Here are the basic parts of an open back banjo, which is the most common type (though not the only type) of instrument being used for old time music today.

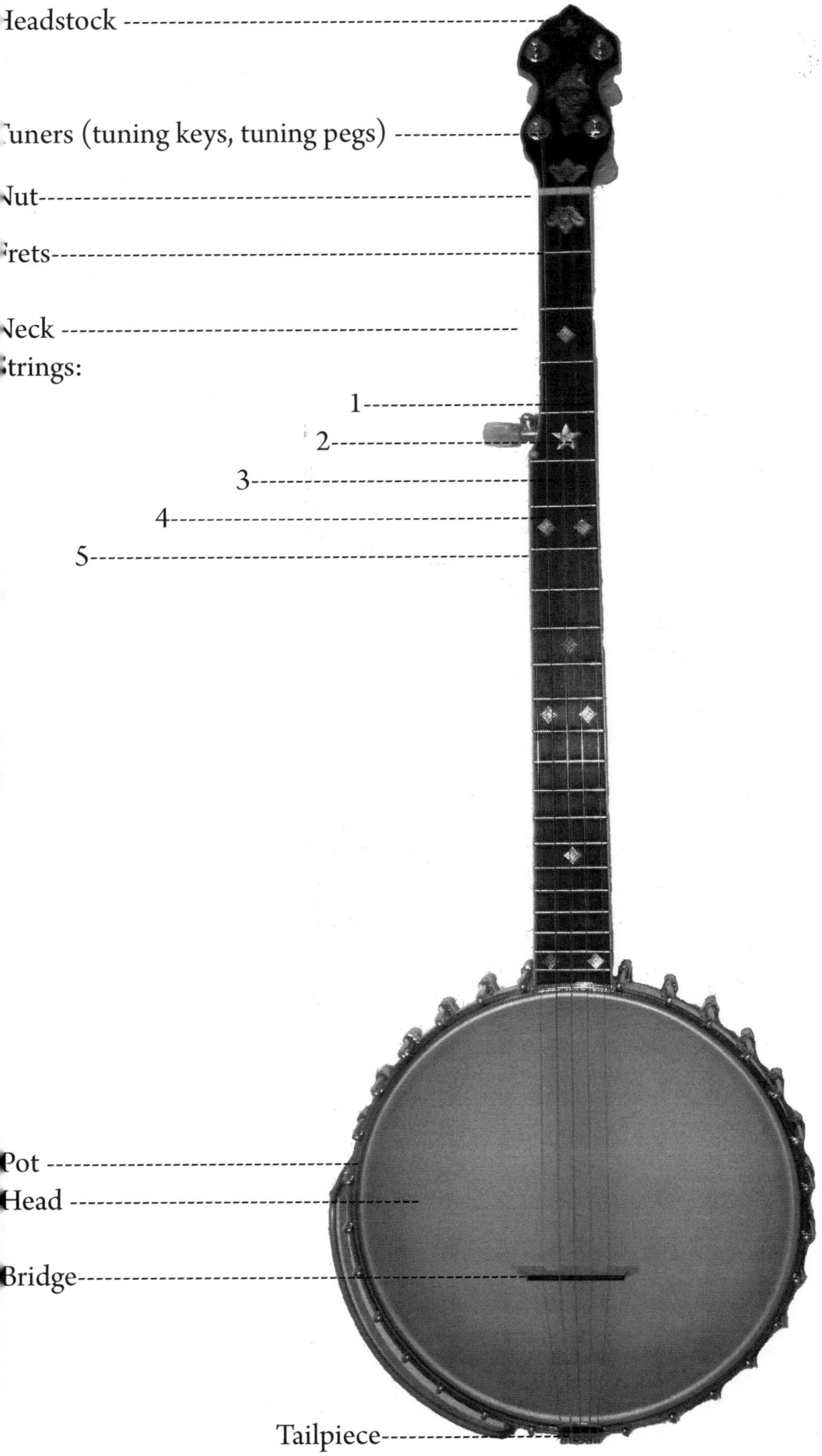

Reading tablature

This book is written in a type of music notation known as tablature. Reading tablature is in many ways easier than reading music. Tablature (tab) was developed to help you read music without really reading music. Huh? Okay, tablature tells you where to place your finger to play a note on your banjo, without actually having to know what note (A, B, C etc.) it is. It does that by indicating what fret on which string you are supposed to put your finger to play a certain note.

In tablature, the lines of the staff indicate the strings of the banjo, and the notes are numbers that tell you which fret number to put your finger on the string. The drawback of tablature is that it does NOT tell you which finger to use.

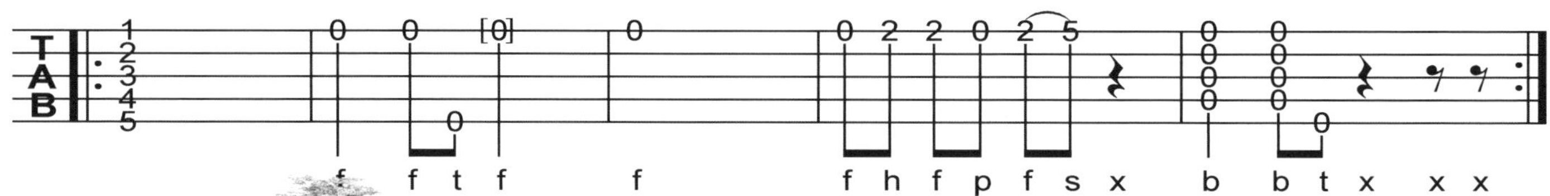

Example 1

In tablature (example 1 - above), the staff is the set of horizontal lines that the notes are written on. The word "TAB" tells you it is tablature. Those two lines (*double bar*) with what looks like a colon next to it, is a *repeat* sign. The beginning repeat has the colon to the right of the double bar, and the ending one has the colon to the left of the double bar. They are used in pairs to indicate that you are supposed to play the phrase that is between them two times through before going on to the next phrase.

Banjo tablature has five horizontal lines per staff. The first measure shows which line represents which string. The "1" on the top line means that line represents the first string of your banjo and the "5" here is telling you the bottom line is the 5th (short) string. This is just something that stays the same, so you won't see the string numbers on regular tab. (FYI, guitar tab would have 6 lines, mandolin tab - 4.)

The second measure shows the notes we use. A quarter note counts as 1 beat (say, "one"). Eighth notes count as 1/2 beat each, so 2 eighth notes = one quarter note (say, "one and"), and a half note counts for 2 beats or 2 times a quarter note (say, "one, two"). The next measure shows a whole note, which counts as 4 beats (say, "one, two, three, four").

The fourth measure shows you a hammer on open string (0) to second fret (2), pull off from the second fret (2) to an open string, a slide from the second (2) to fifth (5) fret with a curved line above them (a *slur*), and a quarter note rest. (More on what these are later in the book). The final measure shows a quarter note, two eighth notes, a quarter note rest, two eighth rests and an ending repeat sign.

Notice the letters under the notes? The f and t indicate whether you use the finger - "f" or the thumb - "t" of your right hand to play the note. The "b" stands for brush across all the strings with your right hand's fingernail. An "x" indicates silence and means that you don't play this note.

The h, p and s give directions for your left hand. The "h" is a hammer-on, the "p" is for a pull-off and the "s" indicates a slide. These are all techniques you will be learning later in this book.

Holding your banjo

You know the song, She came from Alabama with a banjo on her KNEE - (not between her legs, right?) and my position is based upon this. When I sit, I like to hold the banjo on my right "knee" (thigh, actually) with the neck out to the left, pointing out just below my shoulder (see photo). Some folks call this guitar style, and I find this position to be the most natural and comfortable one for me. It is also about the same spot as the banjo hangs from a strap when I stand (see photo), so the bonus is that I don't have to change my playing position or style between sitting and standing.

Let's start here. I think you will find this comfortable as well. Even if you eventually choose another position, this is a good place to start. Like most things, there is no *right* way to do this. I will say that if what you do "hurts" (i.e. causes physical pain), then you may be doing something wrong. Other than that, you can try different things until you find the *right* one for you. BUT, for now, start this way.

Before we go any further, let's take a little time to get your banjo in tune.

Tuning your banjo

Track 1

We are going to tune to what is called G Tuning. The notes you will tune your banjo to are gDGBD from the 5th string to the 1st. Remember, the 5th string is the short one and the top one as you hold the banjo.

For many of you, this may be your first stringed instrument and may even be the first instrument you have ever played. If you have played music before or even have experience with stringed instruments, this part should come easy, so forgive me if we take it a bit slow.

The notes in G tuning are gDGBD from the 5th (short string) to the 1st string. I have provided you reference pitches on the recording that comes with this book. (Tuning reference pitches Track...)

One very popular way to tune is with an electronic tuner. In this method of tuning, you will use the electronic tuner to tell you whether or not you are in tune, and to what note. Basically, you play a string on your banjo into the tuner's microphone, or you clip the tuner to your banjo directly or with a pickup or tuning clip from the tuner attached to your banjo. The tuner electronically reads the note you played, and tells you what note it reads and how sharp (above) or flat (below) your note is compared to the note you want. Each tuner operates differently, so you will have to check the instructions that come with your tuner. Most tell you when you are in tune either by an in tune light, several lights, a centering needle or a combination of the two. They also have some way of telling you what note you have played. Like I said, check the instructions that come with the specific tuner you have.

There are also apps for your phone or iPod that can either read the note you play or generate a sound for the pitch you want so you can tune to it. They are quite handy and convenient, and many are free. I have several, but the latest from Peterson Strobe Tuners is the best one I have found. You can contact them at *www.petersontuners.com* for the most up to date info on this one.

Some tuners have trouble reading (hearing) a banjo's notes because of all the overtones (ringing sounds) from the banjo. This can cause you to get a false reading or sometimes even no reading at all from your tuner. Background noise from talking or other instruments can also make it hard for the tuner to pick out your banjo's note, which is why the tuning clip or direct attachment of the tuner to your banjo usually works better.

If you have not gotten an electronic tuner yet, you should try several before buying one. Take your banjo with you to do this. Check with friends, ask at the store you patronize, or specify to the order taker at the mail order place you deal with that you will be using this for a banjo. If the person you are talking to doesn't know which tuner to recommend, ask if anyone there does, and make sure you can return it if it doesn't work well with your banjo.

Because of the flexible head, banjo tuning is made more difficult since as you tune one string, others can go out of tune. To minimize this problem, I have a pattern I follow when tuning a banjo. Whether you tune to a pitch from the disc or choose to tune to an electronic tuner, tuning fork, a piano or other instrument, I like to tune the strings in this order: 3 - 5 - 1 - 4 - 2 (ie. Tune the 3rd string first, then the 5th, and etc.).

Lets go back to the electronic tuner for now. First, start by playing the third string into the tuner and see what note the tuner says you have played. It should give you a name of the note it reads (i.e. A, B, C...) and an indication of whether the note you played is sharp ("#"- the note is too high) or flat ("b" - the note is too low). This string should be a G. Once you have gotten this G string in tune, go on to the 5th string. This is also a G note, only an octave (8 notes) higher, so you are again looking for the note to be G, and the in tune signal (light or needle) to tell you when you are in tune.

The next string I would tune is the first string. This should be a D. Next go to the 4th string D (yep, an octave below the first string) and finally the 2nd string - B. You can see we are crossing back and forth across the head while tuning. BUT, some movement has occurred, so lets go back. Start again and fine tune the strings once more in the same order, then check them again one more time from 5 to 1 in order. The notes of your banjo strings should now match the reference notes on the audio. Now that we are in tune, let's start playing!

Your first strum - I'm going to break your basic stroke down to two steps. Your *first strum* and then your *basic strum*. The reason for this is to make it easier for you AND to give you a couple of notes about keeping time.

I like to think of the hand as a unit, so you strum down once for each word that will be one beat for each strum. (Beat? Huh? Just a minute, first things first). I like to use my middle fingernail to strum the notes but others prefer the index finger. Don't worry about which one to use. Just pick one for now.

As your hand strums or "brushes" or "strokes" the four melody (long) strings, the thumb should come to rest on the fifth (short) string. Don't worry when you start this process because it will often miss and hit another or even no string. Just relax and keep the hand as a unit as it drops across the strings for the down-stroke.

I hold my hand at about a 45-60 degree angle to the head of the banjo, and I aim for striking across the strings with the 10 o'clock position of the nail. I use it something like a guitar pick to strum the strings while my hand is going down towards the floor for the stroke (see photo).

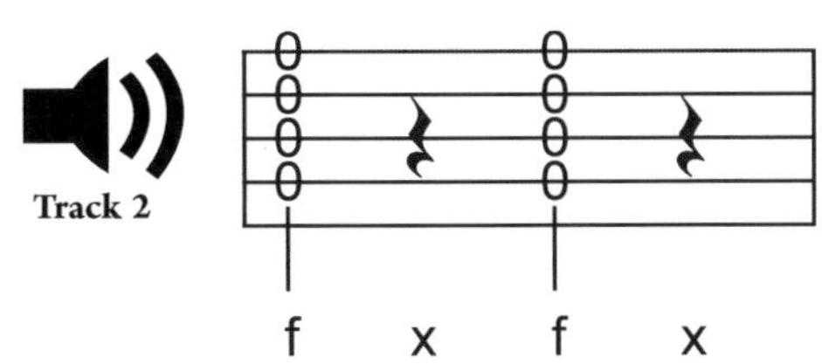

Example 2

As you lift your hand back to your starting position, the thumb can and may "catch" just behind the fifth string (head side of the string and from the top) sounding it in a very natural way. Again, it may not when you start, so for now no worries, don't obess on it, just get used to the gentle hand motion of stroking down with the fingernail and catching up with the thumb. One down stroke per beat, one strum, one stroke (example 2). Down–brush the strings, Up–silent, recover the hand to the starting position. Drop/Lift/Drop/Lift and repeat...***Remember:***

LET IT HAPPEN, DON'T MAKE IT HAPPEN

Row, Row, Row, Your Boat – I

Track 3

It's time to play a tune!

Let's start with a well know favorite that I'm sure you already know. *Row, Row, Row, Your Boat.* You know this one, "Row row row your boat gently down the stream". If you strum your banjo once for each word, you will have the basic idea of how your hand works. Remember to lift your hand back to its starting position before each note.

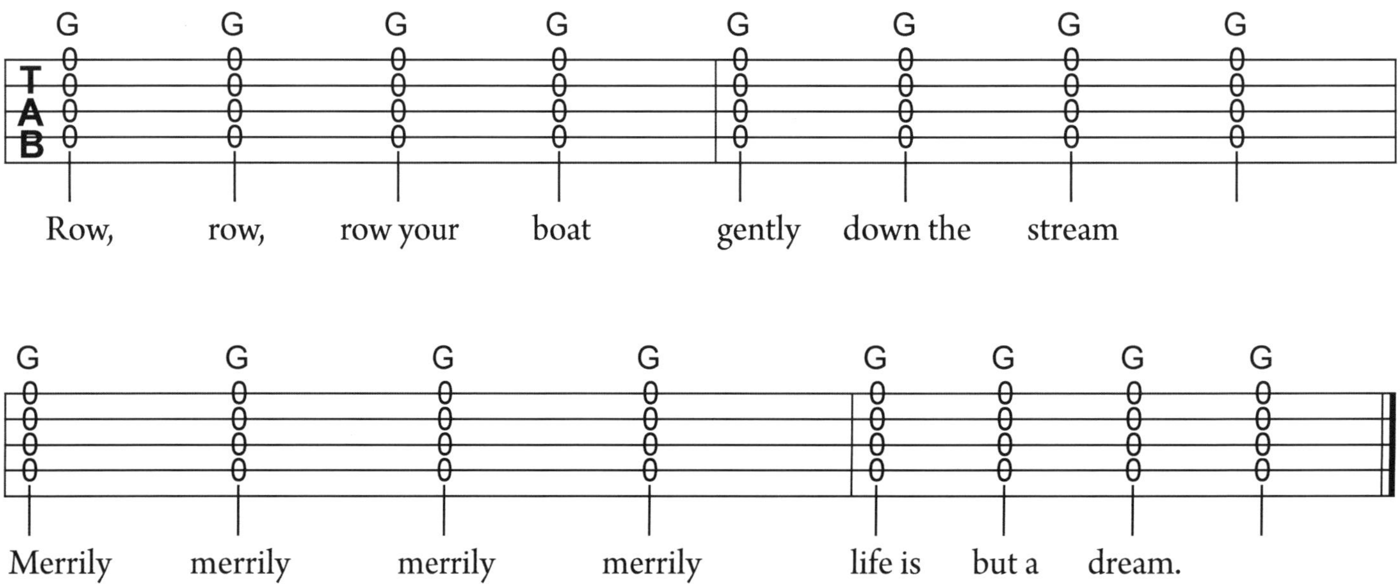

And you're off and rowing... I mean sailing...! Gently down the stream of playing folk music. You've worked hard! I wouldn't blame you if you just wanted to take a break now and go sailing yourself. SO, take a bit and when you come back we'll talk about timing.

"Stroke, stroke, stroke, stroke" (hey, that's a lot like what we just did!)

Timing and keeping time with the metronome

Keeping time means playing your music evenly and so other folks can stay with you. That means evenly counting time, which for most folks takes a bit of practice AND a guide to keep them in time. I don't mean tapping your foot here either. Keeping time is an acquired skill and in order to develop it you need some reliable source of the beat that is not influenced by your belief of being in time or other outside forces. Another way to say this is that if you can't keep time with your hands (yet), your foot doesn't do any better. What you need is called a metronome.

The *metronome* is not a little urban up to date fancy dresser! It's a device that keeps time for you. It can be mechanical, requiring you to wind it up, or electronic - battery operated or plugged in. It makes a noise and or blinks a light at regular intervals. Some even come with earphones.

You set the time in the number of beats per minute (bpm) and then each click, beep or flash of the light counts as one beat. If you set the metronome for 100 bpm, the metronome will tick (or flash a light) 100 times every minute. That means that if you are playing quarter notes, you would play one note per click. If you are playing eighth notes, that would be 2 notes per click, and so on. While it may SEEM like a Chinese torture device, and it is inflexible and unforgiving, a metronome will keep solid time as long as you want! (Well, at least until the batteries run out or the spring winds down.)

The first thing folks discover when using a metronome is that you paid a lot of money for a device that doesn't seem to keep time any better than you do. BUT, after working with it for a while, you'll swear the darn thing figured out how you play and keeps time with *you*!

I know folks like to think that tapping the foot is an adequate substitute for a metronome. My experience and the studies of this method have shown that it does NOT work. The reason for this is simple. Your foot tapping is controlled by your internal rhythm. Good internal rhythm is something that most folks need to develop, and the metronome is the best way to get it. Remember:

If you can't keep time with your hand, your foot can't possibly be doing any better!

In addition, the foot really makes noise and can be pretty loud and distracting, especially when it is amplified by a microphone, stage and sound system. If you just gotta move something, try your head. Smile, bob and dance your head, but play without tapping your foot.

Now, try to *Row Your Boat* again with that ol tippy tappy metronome counting time for you.

Say, did you notice that the last part of that tune didn't sound quite right? Yes, that is because you were missing a *chord*. A what? A chord. "What's a chord" you ask? Well, I'll tell ya!

Chords and fretting the notes

Webster's New World Dictionary defines a *chord* as "...a combination of three or more tones sounded together in harmony...". Without getting too technical, chords give you a very nice, full sound and are great for backing up a tune, especially if you want to accompany singing. Chords are comprised of a root, third and fifth of a particular scale played together. In the case of the of G chord, the notes would be G (root note of the G chord), a B (3rd note of the G chord), and D (5th note of the G chord). Played together, they make a full G chord. Hey! Those are the notes our banjo is tuned to right now! And that means you are ahead of the game right from the start! You already know and are playing your G chord. BUT, you are not done yet.

In order to play most basic folk songs you need one or two more chords. If we consider the G chord the I (roman numeral 1) chord, we need a IV and a V chord to get going further gently down the stream of playing folk music with a banjo. And when I call them I, IV and V that means that they are the first, fourth and fifth chords of the scale. The key again is G, so G is the I chord. That means the other two chords for this key will be C (G, A, B, C – IV) and D (G, A, B, C, D – V), well actually a D7 chord, but lets not get into that now okay?

Your banjo is already tuned to a G chord – gDGBD. Put in chord terms, open 4th string (D – the 5th), open 3rd string (G – the root), open 2nd (B – the third), and the open first string (D – another 5th) and of course, our fifth string – g (another root).

Making the other chords – In order to play the other chords you need, you have to fret the strings – or press down the string near the fret – in order to change the pitch of each string to get the notes you want to make your chords. To do this, you place a finger of your left hand down on a string just behind (to the headstock side of) the fret (metal bar) for each note you want to play (see photo).

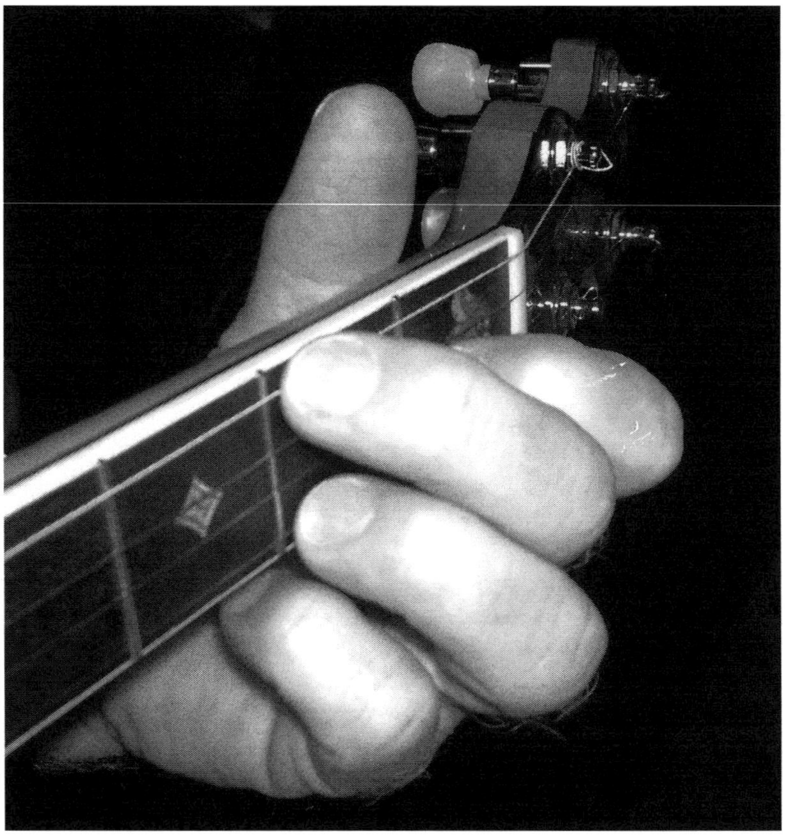

A student asks, "Which fingers do I use on my left hand to make the chords?" As I mentioned earlier, one drawback of tablature is that it tells you which fret to put your finger at, but not which finger to use. For now, I'll tell you. For the G chord, great news, no fingers down!

For the C – or IV chord, the tab shows a 2nd fret on the 1st string, a 1st fret on the 2nd string, an open (0) third string and a 2nd fret on the 4th string.

Start by placing your 1st finger at the 1st fret of the 2nd string, your 2nd finger at the 2nd fret of the 4th string and put your 3rd finger at the 2nd fret of the first string.

Start by using the tip of your finger for this as it is more accurate, and you will need less pressure to get a clean note. As you can see in the photo, you have the neck of your banjo in your left hand parallel with the lifeline in that hand, and the thumb joint on the back of the neck just on or above the curve of the neck, pointing up (parallel or almost parallel to the frets). One way to get this is by making a circle with the finger and thumb, then put the banjo in place where the finger touches the thumb.

This allows you to curl your fingers so you can place your fingertip on the string just behind (the headstock side of) the metal fret. Press down only on the string you are fretting with only enough pressure to get a clear sounding note.

Too much pressure, and you might notice your fingernail turning white. This will push the note out of tune, hurt your fingers and hasten the wear on your instrument's frets and fingerboard. Too little pressure, and you will only get a dull, thuddy note.

Also, be sure to come down straight and clean on only ONE string, or you will be deadening the one(s) next to it. The object here is to get a clean note on one string.

Try putting each finger down one at a time and sound it as a clear note before adding the next finger.

Once you have the whole C chord in place and all of the notes clear, let your right hand playing finger brush across all of the strings with the chord held down. Now lift the fingers just a bit and brush the open (G) chord, then the C chord, open, C, open until you can just put the chord down clean without watching your hand.

Now for your D7 – or V chord. Put the 1st finger on the 1st fret of the 2nd string, and the 2nd finger at the 2nd fret of the 3rd string. Repeat the process you did with the C chord of putting each finger down one at a time until you have a clean chord. Then play with the chord then without it, on, off, on, off (D7, G, D7, G) until it is also clean and you can put the chord down without looking.

Example 3 shows each chord written in tablature. Try strumming each one.

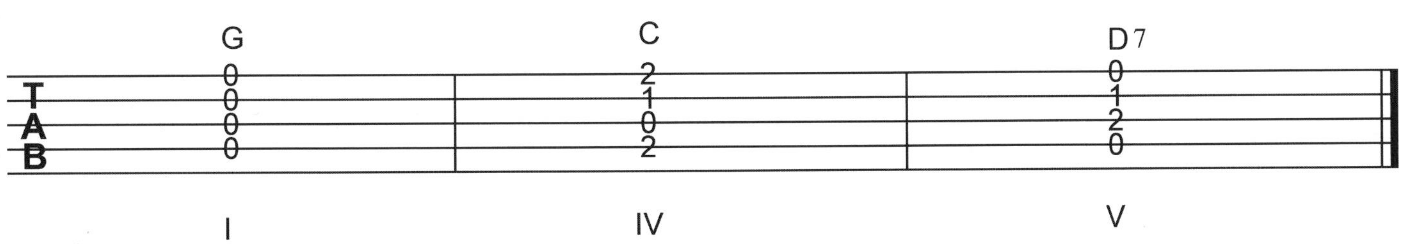

Example 3

HELPFUL HINT! If you only lift the fingers until they are off the string, but still hovering over the fingerboard and strings, you won't get out of position with that one chord or travel too far to change chords when it comes time to switch from one chord to another.

Here's an exercise so you can get comfortable with each chord, then going from one chord to another, then through the entire I-IV-V or G-C-D7 pattern, because that is what you will be doing for many of your tunes.

Track 5

I - IV

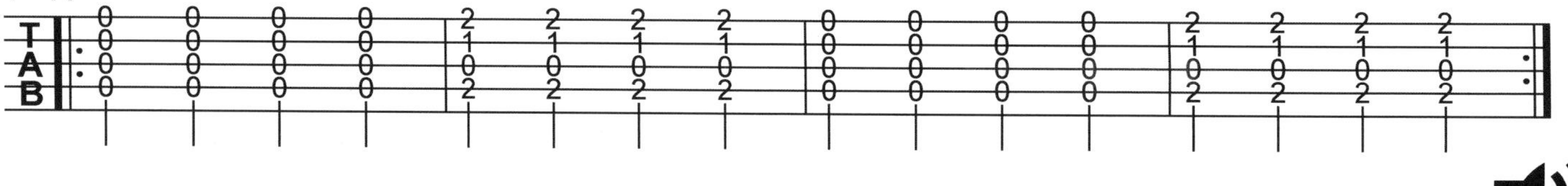

Track 6

I - V

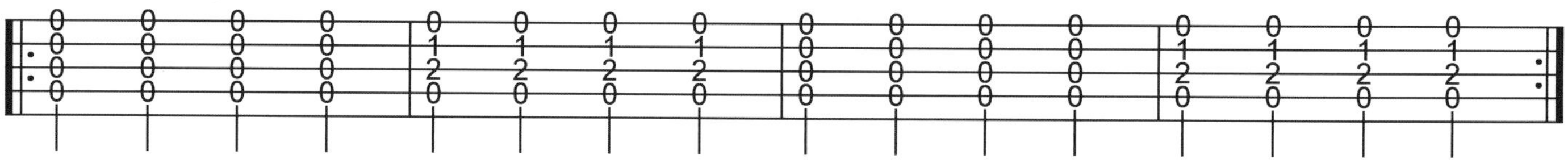

Track 7

IV - V

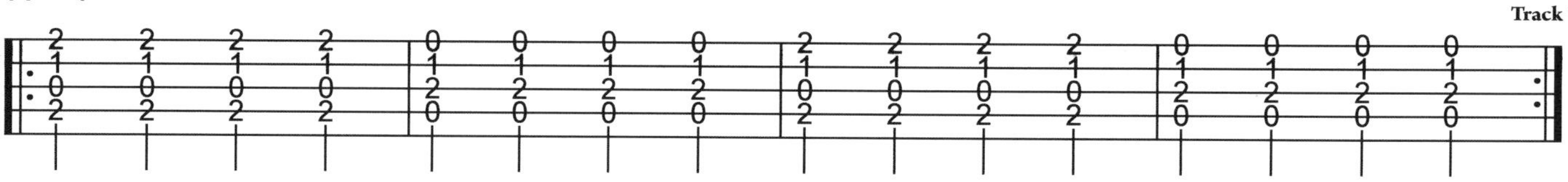

Track 8

I - IV - V - I

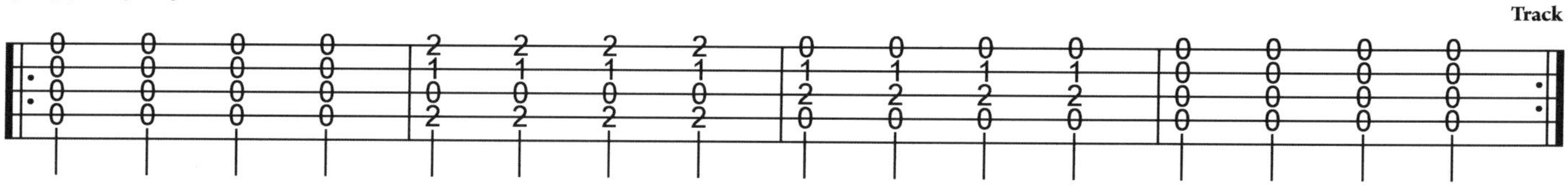

Track 9

I - IV - I - V - I - IV - V - I

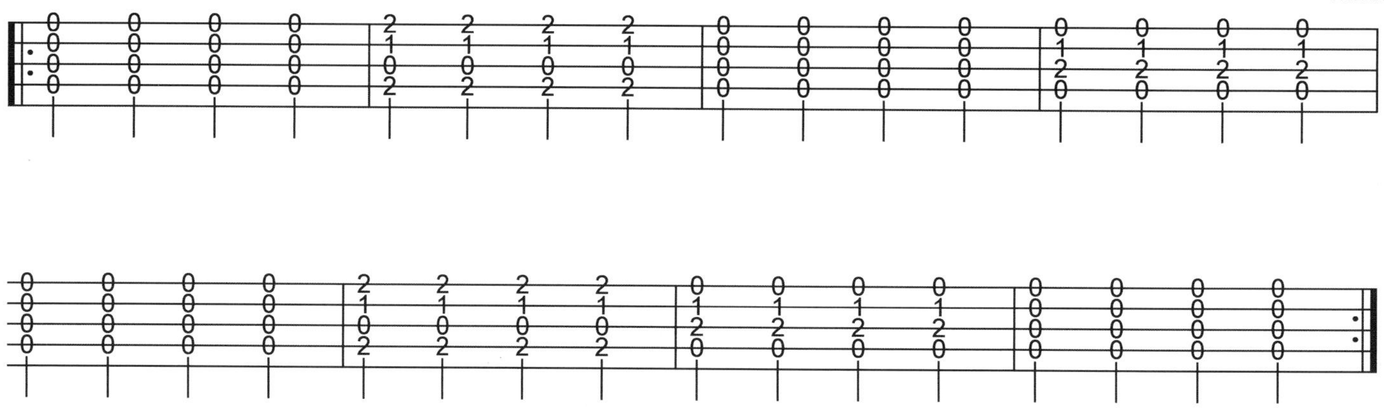

Example 4

These chord changes should all be smooth before continuing on to the tune.

Row, Row, Row Your Boat – II

Track 10

Your First Tune – Row–visited

Let's start to put this into practice with adding just one chord - the D7 (V) chord at the end of Row, Row, Row Your Boat. Listen to how nice just this small addition of that one chord sounds, and how much change can come from such a small change.

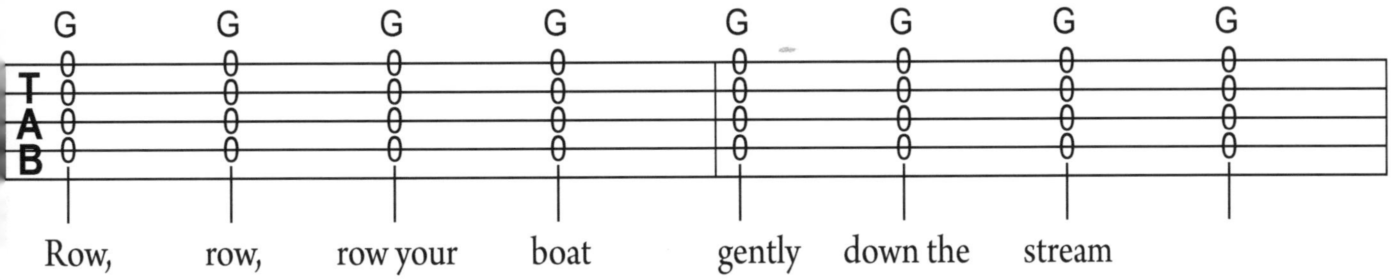

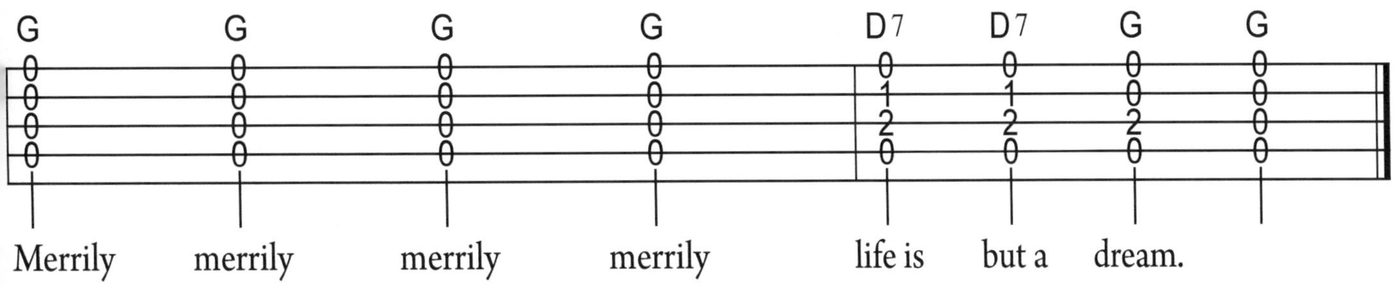

You have done a great job today. Good work here, so you may just want to take a breather before adding the next step.

THUMBS UP! The Basic Stroke

Okay now, let's add the thumb and complete our *basic stroke*! Up to this point, I have only briefly mentioned the thumb part of the stroke, but now I want to concentrate on it. We are going to sound the thumb on every stroke.

For each finger stroke down, there is a thumb plucking up. Well, actually the thumb sounds as the *hand* comes up. As your hand comes down for the strum, the thumb slips just behind (the head side of) the fifth string (see photo). SO, as you LIFT your hand, the thumb catches the fifth string and sounds it as you lift your hand and recover back to your starting position.

Let's go step by step. The hand drops with the finger brushing the strings (remember only strings 4-1) as the thumb lands on the fifth string. As you lift your hand up, the thumb plucks, or more accurately "catches" the fifth string sounding it as the hand lifts. This divides each beat into two halves, which are shown by eighth notes, and allows you to get sound on both the front and back of the beat.

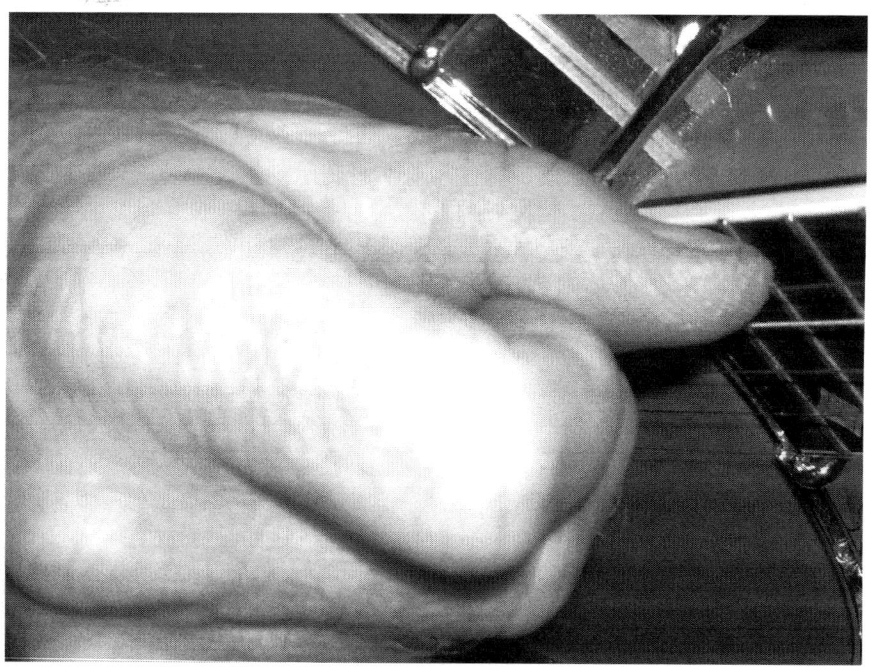

Track 11

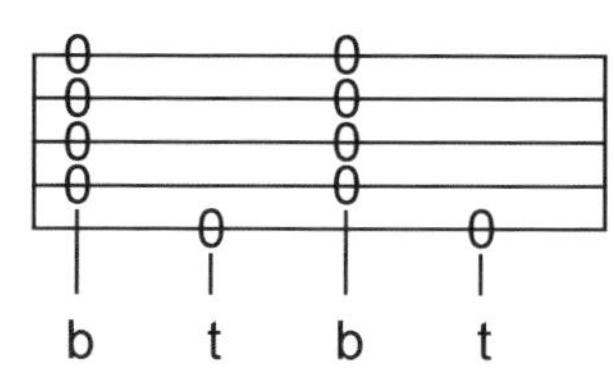

Example 5

First, let's do it with quarter notes. Each note is one beat. This means that for each click of the metronome (you are using it right?) you get one beat and one direction of your hand. Click 1 - hand down - strum the chord as the thumb lands on top of and just slips slightly behind the fifth string, click 2 - the hand lifts and the thumb catches and sounds the fifth string as written out here in example 5. Cool huh? And no work, either. Remember to move from the wrist joint, not the elbow or the finger or thumb.

Track 12

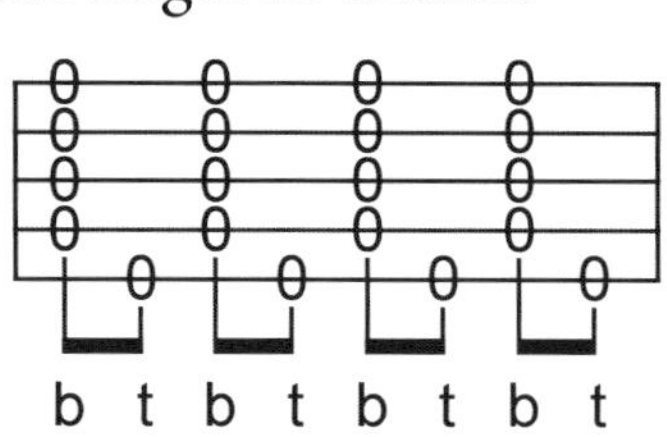

Example 6

Now, let's cut each note in half. Instead of one note per click, you get two, BUT it still comes in the time it takes for one beat. Now you lift your hand and the thumb sounds! Example 6 shows how this looks written out in tab.

Basic Stroke Chord Exercise

Now let's just combine the basic stroke with the chord exercise

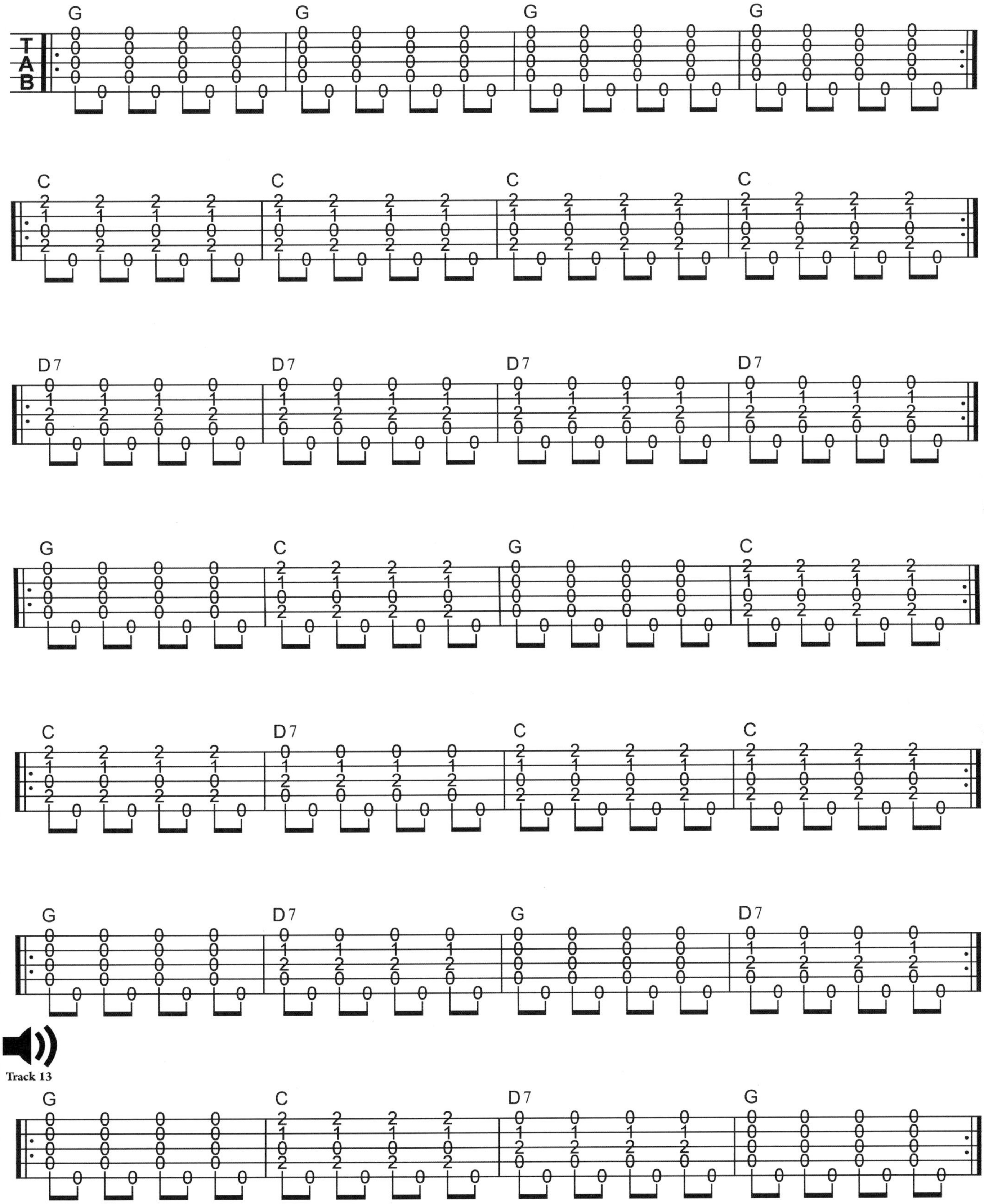

Example 7

Row, Row, Row Your Boat – III

Track 14

Now Row along with me just one more time! Row Row ROW Your Boat —this time with with chord change and thumb

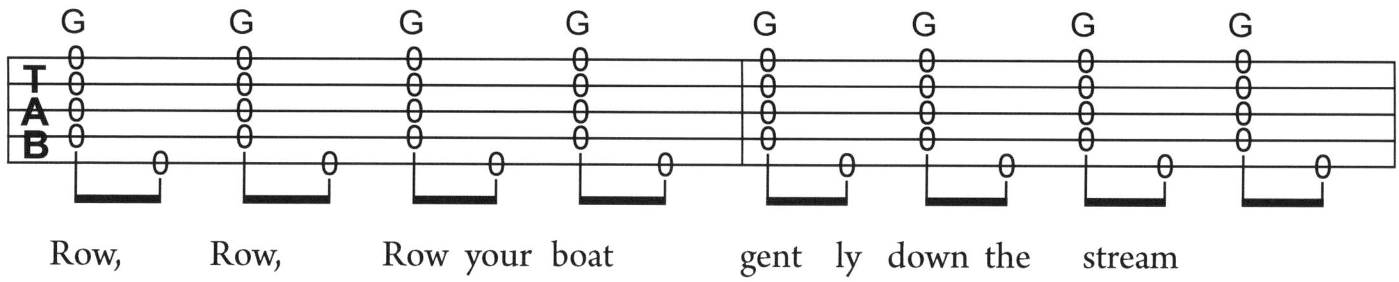

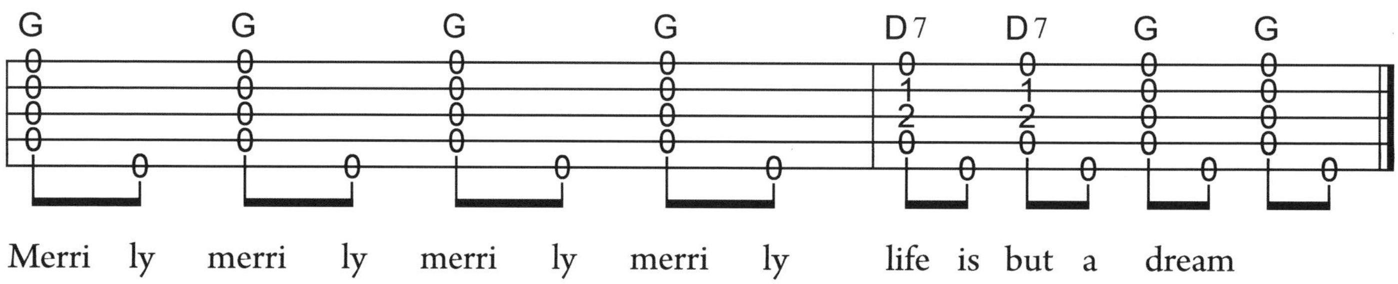

Notice how the words lay out once we add the back beats (the *and*) to the strum and the tune. As you play it this time, here are questions you can be asking yourself as you work on this tune in its final form.

Is my arm and hand in a comfortable position? Is it where it goes, or is it where I think it "should" be?

Is my thumb resting slightly pointed into (and somewhat behind) the fifth (short) string? Can I see the knuckle of my ring (third) finger?

Remember, I use my MIDDLE finger 'kauz it sounds bestest! BUT you get to choose! So I bring the EDGE of the edge of my middle fingernail to the strings.

Let the hand fall for the down beat strum (or brush stroke), then lift the hand to sound the thumb.

Repeat slowly enough to remember to put the D7 down at the word "life", but fast enough to sound like a song. Keep the flow and don't play too fast, but aim for not too slow either.

Starting speed set my metronome at 50 and one full stroke/thumb per click. Brush on each click.

Ask yourself, "are my wrists and hands relaxed, are my notes clean and the chord as clean sounding as the open strings? Do I notice ANY tension or muddy notes, do I need to listen and relax more?"

Do the same for this tune and all exercises (like the chord change exercise) and tunes.

LETS PLAY SOME MUSIC AND SING SOME SONGS!

Little Brown Jug

chord changes with basic stroke and the original words from 1869!

Track 15

Key of G
G tuning – gDGBD

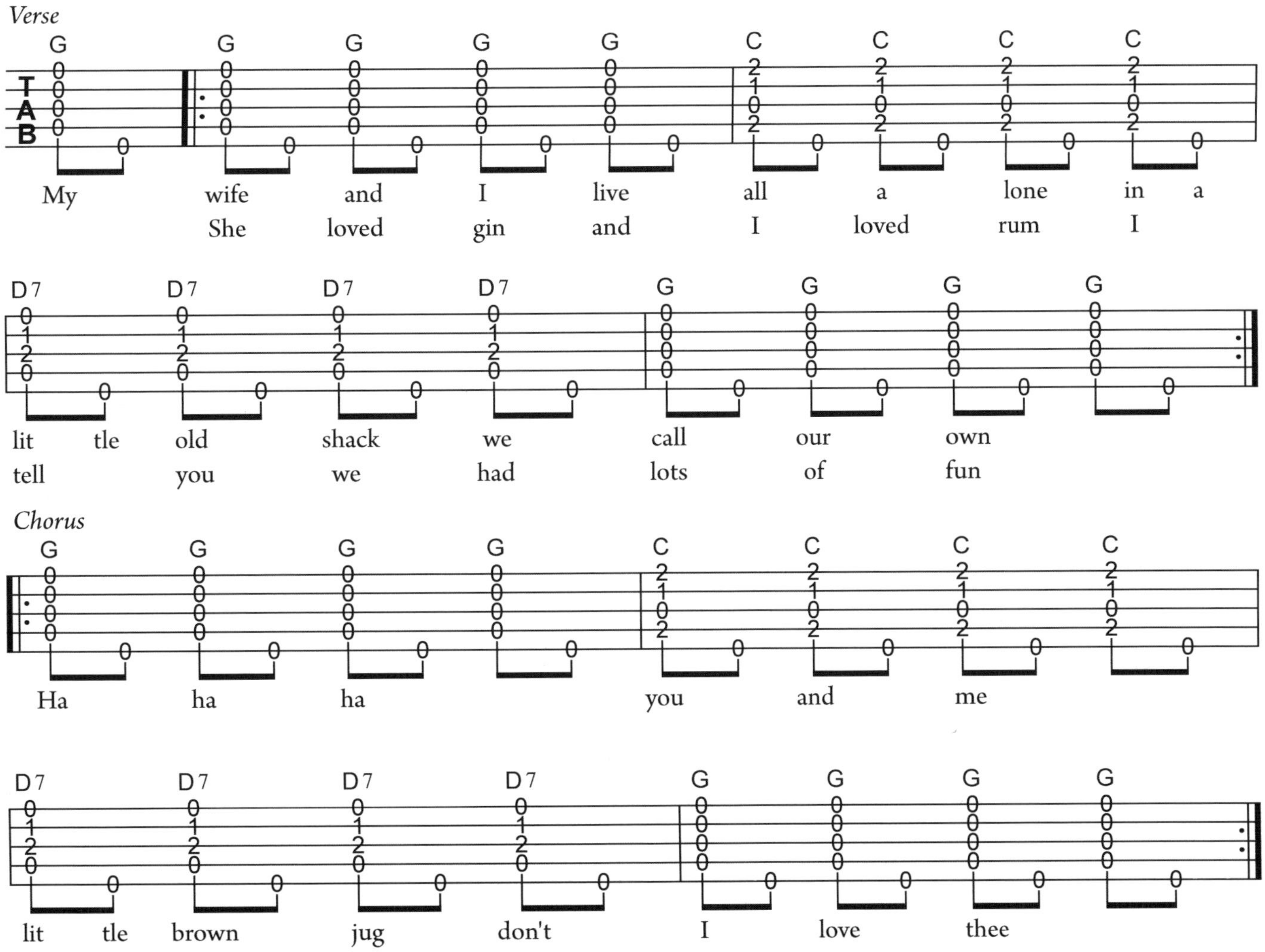

My wife and I live all alone, in a little old shack we call our own;
She loved gin and I loved rum, I tell you we had lots of fun.

Chorus: Ha, ha, ha, you and me, Little Brown Jug don't I love thee;
Ha, ha, ha, you and me, Little Brown Jug don't I love thee.

If all the folks in Adam's race, Were gathered together in one place;
Then I'd prepare to shed a tear, Before I'd part from you, my dear.

'Tis you who makes my friends my foes, 'Tis you who makes me wear old clothes;
Here you are, so near my nose, So tip her up, and down she goes.

If I'd a cow that gave such milk, I'd clothe her in the finest silk;
I'd feed her on the choicest hay, And milk her forty times a day.

When I go toiling to my farm, I take little Brown Jug under my arm;
I place it under a shady tree, Little Brown Jug, 'tis you and me.

The rose is red, my nose is, too, The violet's blue, and so are you;
And yet I guess before I stop, We'd better take another drop.

Cripple Creek—I

Track 16

Key of G
G tuning – gDGBD

Verse

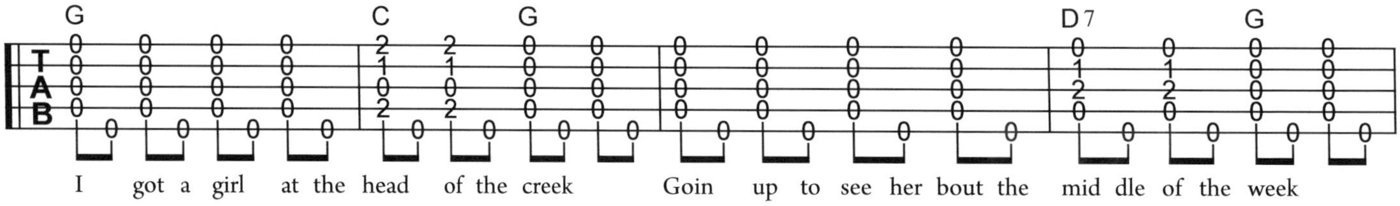

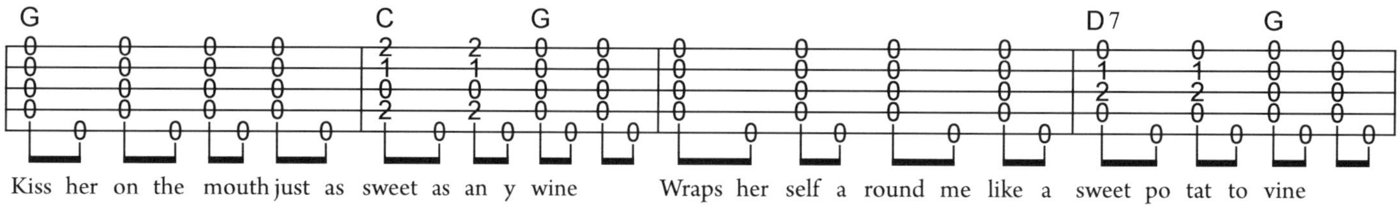

Chorus

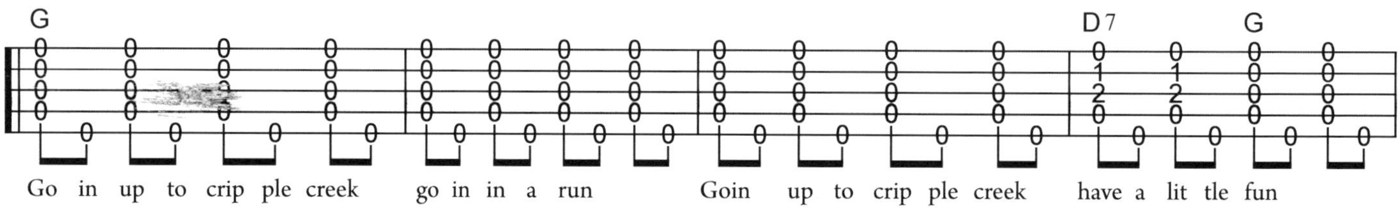

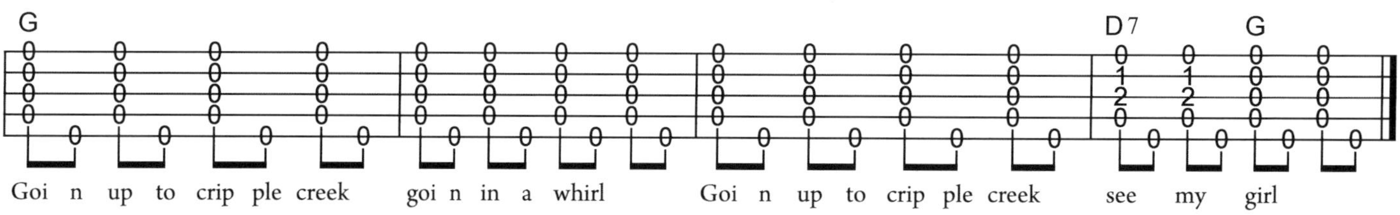

I got a gal at the head of the creek
Goin up t' see her 'bout the middle of the week
Kiss her on the mouth, just as sweet as any wine
Wraps herself around me like a sweet potato vine

Goin' up t' Cripple Creek, goin' on the run
Goin' up t' Cripple Creek t' have a little fun
Goin' up t' Cripple Creek, goin in a whirl
Goin' up t' Cripple Creek t' see my girl

Girls up on Cripple Creek about half grown
Jump on a man like a dog on a bone
I'll roll my britches up to my knees
An' wade in ol' Cripple Creek when I please

Goin' up t' Cripple Creek, goin' on the run
Goin' up t' Cripple Creek t' have a little fun
Goin' up t' Cripple Creek, goin in a whirl
Goin' up t' Cripple Creek t' see my girl

Sourwood Mountain

Track 17

Key of G
G tuning – gDGBD

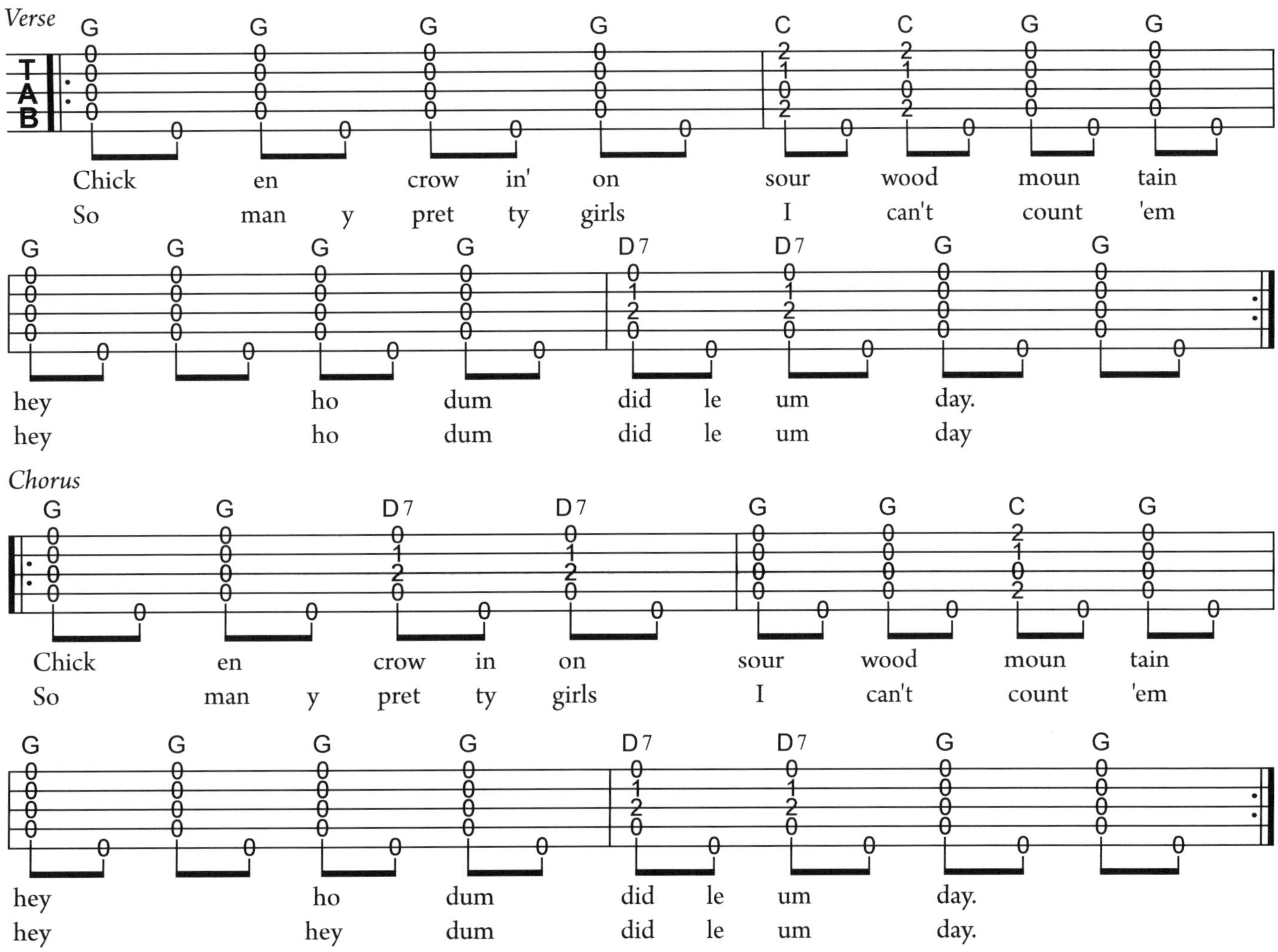

Chickens a crowin' in the Sourwood Mountains
Hey, ho dum diddle um day
So many pretty girls I can't count em
Hey, ho dum diddle um day

My true love's a blue-eyed daisy,
Hey, ho dum diddle um day
If I don't get her, I'll go crazy.
Hey, ho dum diddle um day

Say old man I want your daughter
Hey, ho dum diddle um day
Bake some bread carry in the water
Hey, ho dum diddle um day

My true love's a blue-eyed daisy,
Hey, ho dum diddle um day
She won't come and I'm too lazy.
Hey, ho dum diddle um day

Big dog bark, little dog bite you
Hey, ho dum diddle um day
Big girl courts, little ones spite you
Hey, ho dum diddle um day

My true love lives up the hollow
Hey, ho dum diddle um day
She won't come and I won't follow
Hey, ho dum diddle um day

My true love lives up on the river
Hey, ho dum diddle um day
A few more miles and I'll be with her
Hey, ho dum diddle um day

Ducks in the mill pond, geese in the clover
Hey, ho dum diddle um day
Tell them pretty girls, I'm a'comin over
Hey, ho dum diddle um day

Let's find us some single notes!

While we can strum and strum–thumb our way through almost any tune – and that is a good way to start learning a new one – you start to make noises more like music once you start adding some melody notes. To do that, your hand has to start to learn where each string is and make it sound by itself. Fortunately, (or perhaps not so fortunately) there are two ways to pick a single note.

First, my preferred method of playing – down picking my single notes. This way doesn't really change what you have been doing so far, so much as make it more accurate.

Here we go. Since you are already stroking down with your hand, letting your finger brush over all the strings, (and letting your thumb catch that fifth string on the upward hand stroke) you have the motion. Now I would like you to MISS all of the strings EXCEPT the first string (long one closest to the floor on your banjo) and strike the first string with your fingernail as your hand makes its downstroke. Next, just hit the second string, then the third string, and then, yes the fourth string. Also, even though I have not written the 5th string into the tab, if you let the thumb land on the fifth string and even sound now and then, no worries.

The tab on the next page shows a full line of each string for practice. Repeat each line until each string is clear and the notes even. Once they are clean, move on to the last three lines. They make you go from one string to the next for every note. You can do this with open strings (a G or I chord) or while making any other chord (your C - IV or D7 - V) to hear how just changing a chord makes a difference in sound, even without changing the exercise! Hey, what can I say, I tend to get bored with exercises, so I like to change em up now and then.

"But Dan, you said there was another way! Maybe it is easier?" Okay, okay, I'll fill yall in. A lot of folks like to actually pick their single note by pulling up on the string instead of dropping their hand to strike it with their nail. Huh? Yep, just pick the first string with your finger by plucking it from below the string instead of striking from above. It is more of a finger picking style when you do it this way, but many folks find it a bit easier. This method has often been called up-picking or "Seeger Style" banjo. It is the style that Pete Seeger plays, learned and taught, and is still played today by many others – especially those who learned from Pete's famous old "Red Book". Though he didn't invent it, Pete, more than others, is credited with bringing this style of playing into the forefront of today's banjo players.

You may notice that by picking up instead of stroking down, your hand doesn't provide the core of the stroke. This becomes more of a finger picking motion, which now comes before the hand drop and lift you have already been working on.

NOTE OF POSSIBLE CONCERN – If you plan on continuing into more fiddle tune styles of playing old time clawhammer banjo, this up–picking style may be a bit of a roadblock when you want to learn some of the advanced clawhammer techniques. For now, it will work just fine, and can continue to do so for many years to come. Don't stress here, though. Just take a moment and pick a method to start with. You may even choose to use both at different times, but for now, just choose one. We won't dwell on the differences any more. The note sequence in this exercise is the same either way.

Finger to Individual Strings

First String

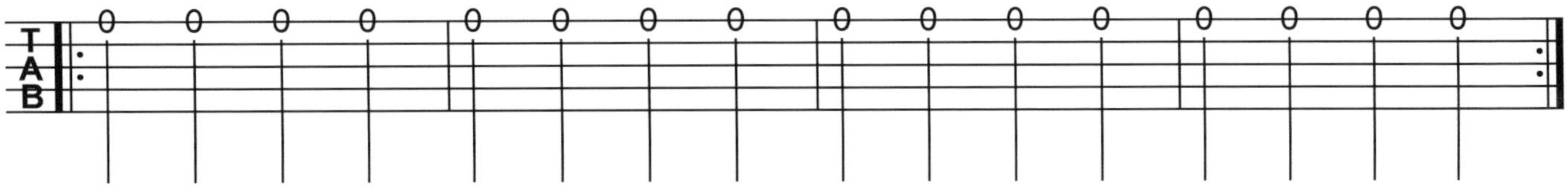

Second String

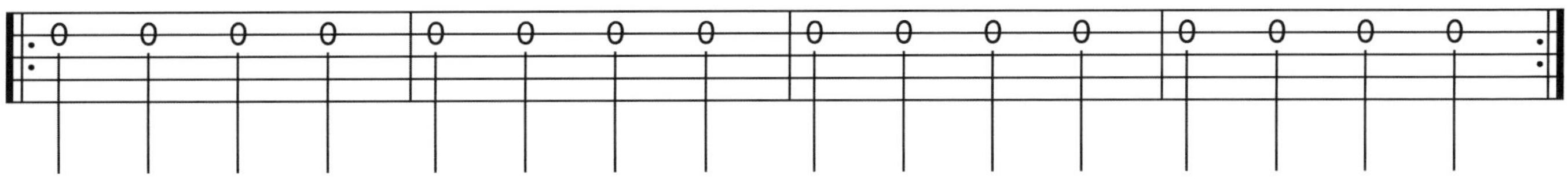

Third String

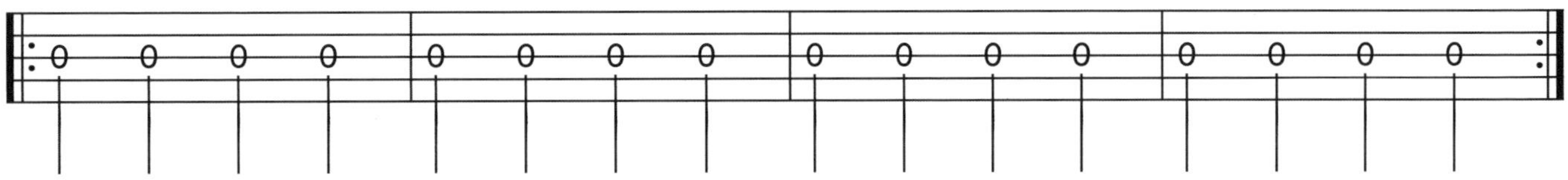

Fourth String

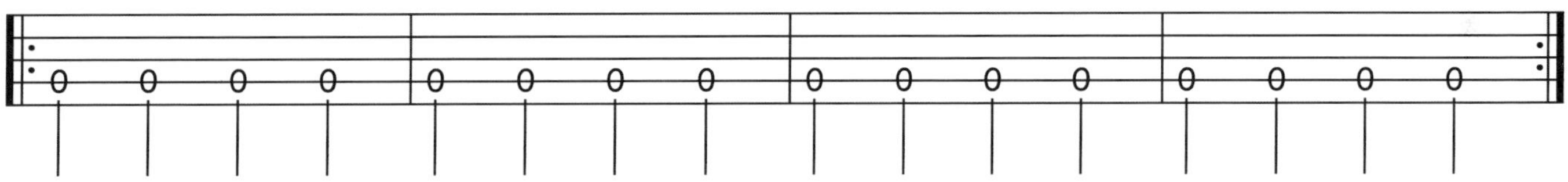

First to fourth string - down

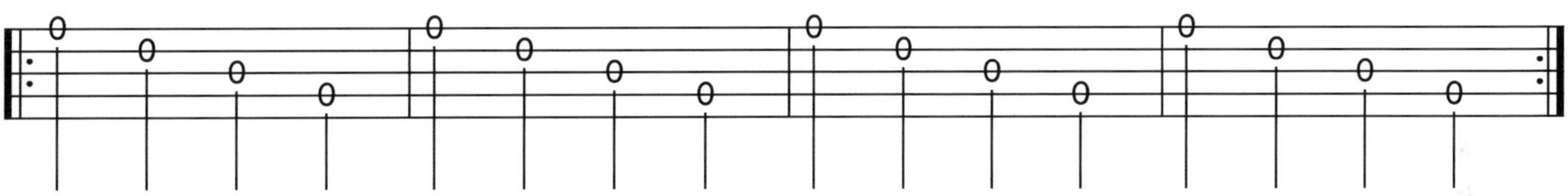

Fourth to first string - up

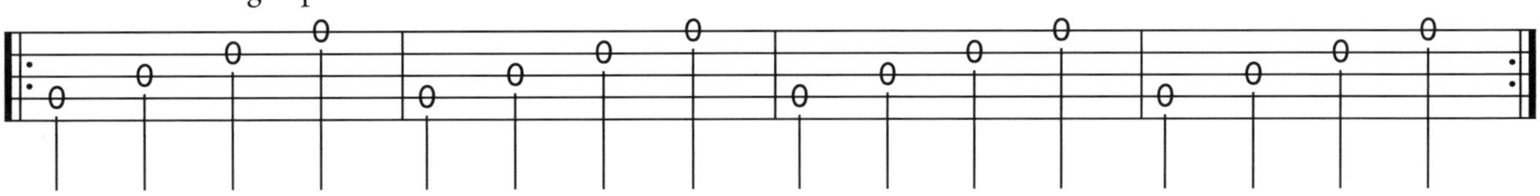

Track 18

First to fourth to first string - down then up   Fourth to first to fourth string - up then down

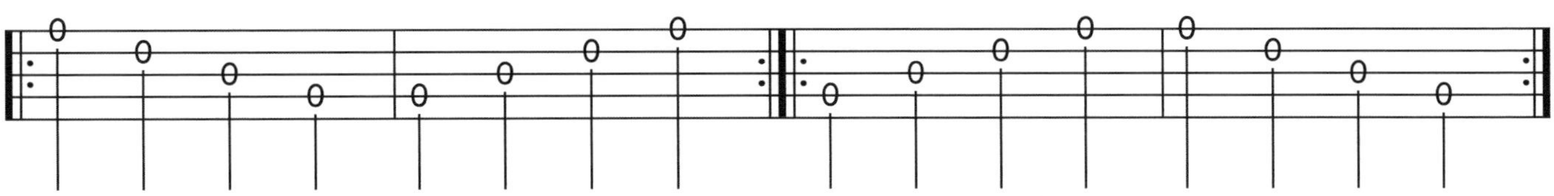

Example 8

A Basic Rhythm - Pick/strum/thumb

Often called the *Bum Diddy,* this is what Pete Seeger called a *Basic Strum* and what I call a *Basic Rhythm*. It is comprised of a finger playing a single note, followed by a strum of the chord, then a thumb pluck. If you are doing all down strokes for your single and chorded notes, this will result in a two part hand motion: down and up where the down stroke hits a single string on the first down of your hand, thumb hits the fifth string but stays SILENT as you lift your hand, then brush the strings with your finger on the next downward stroke of your hand, and this time catch and sound the thumb as you lift your hand. Don't worry if it sounds when you don't want it to and/or doesn't sound when you do. Variety is the spice of banjo and practice will allow you to get the sounds when you want them and not get sound when you don't. It will come.

If you are using the up–pick method here, the motion becomes a three part motion instead of two. The finger plucks the note as the hand lifts up, then the finger brushes down for the chord, and finally the thumb plucks the fifth string. Here is how each chord looks written out in tab with you playing the first string as the single note.

Track 19

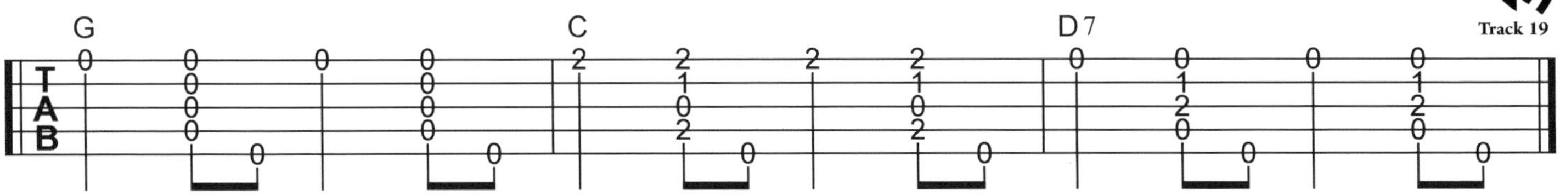

Example 9

Combining the bits: Now let's put all of that hard work to use. It is when you mix the finger strike and follow it with a strum thumb that the joy of this starts to become musical, and some of these little exercises start to make sense. When you start to vary or use a different string for the single note, things REALLY start to change. Here is a tab that does this for each chord. Create your own chord progression exercise (ie: I-IV-V; I-IV-I-V-I-IV-V-I) to set the technique in your hands, as well as the sound in your head.

Track 20-22

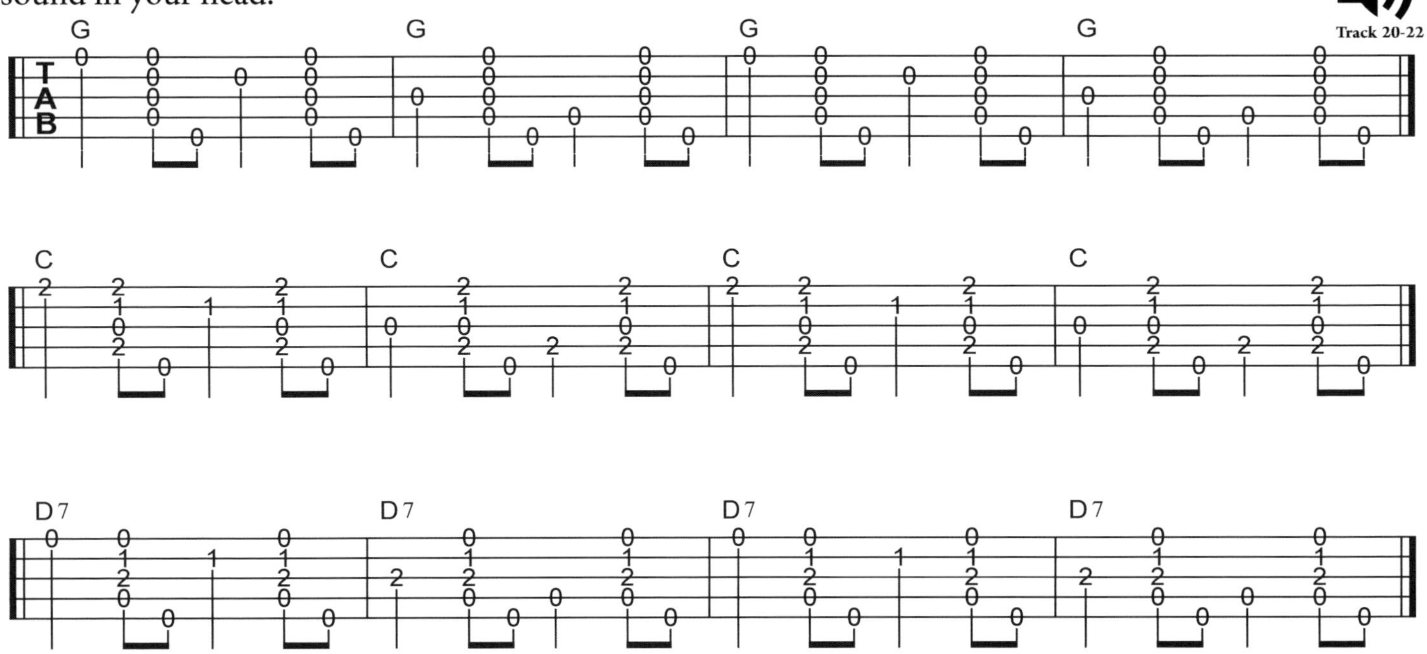

Example 10

Let's play a couple of tunes this way.

Black Eyed Suzie

Track 23

Key of G
G tuning – gDGBD

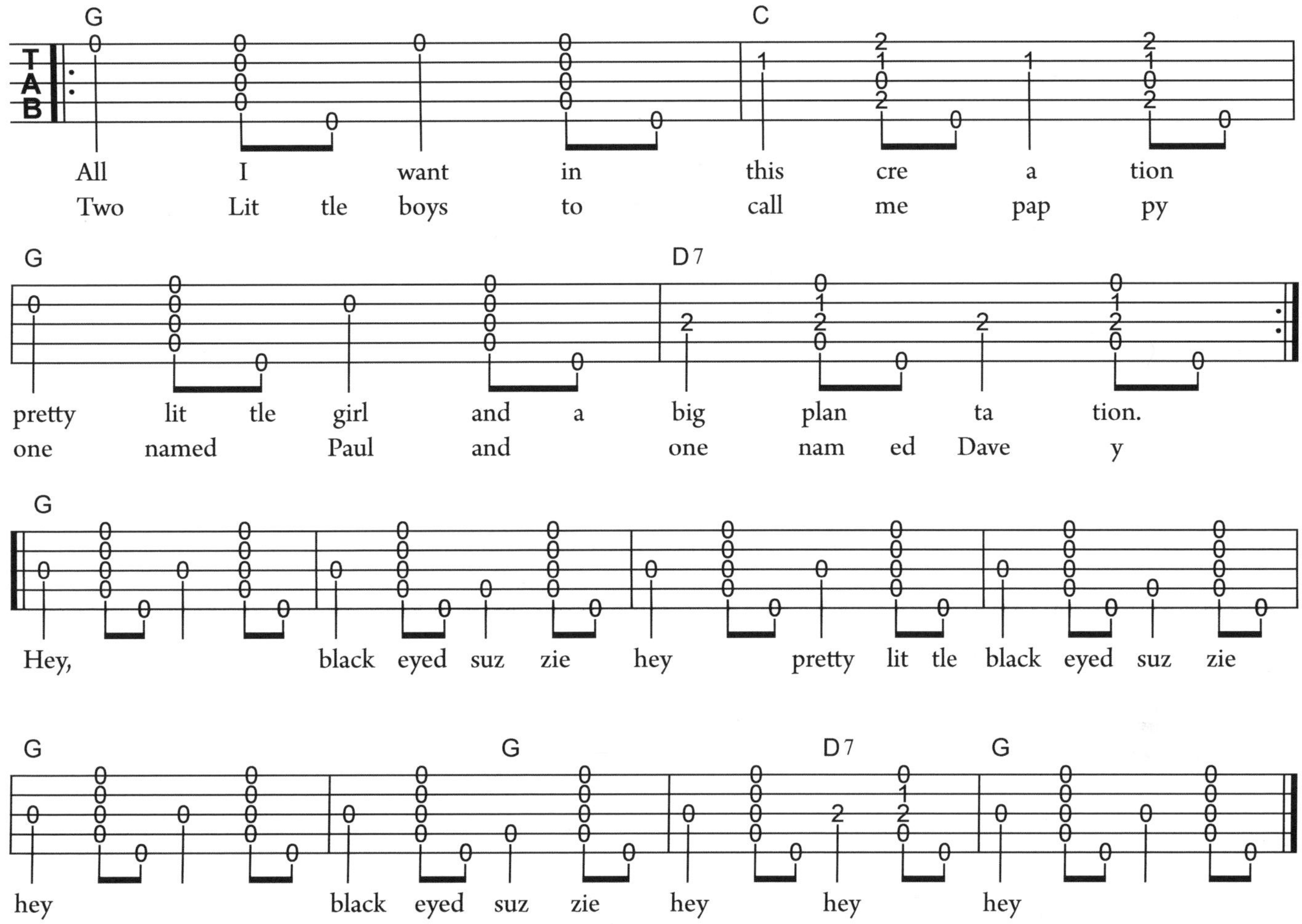

There are a lot of different verses to this one, but these are a few I remember from my childhood.

Black Eyed Suzie's about full grown,
She jumps on a man like a dog on a bone.

Black Eyed Susie went a-huckleberry pickin'
Susie got drunk and the boys took a lickin'.

Chorus:
Hey, black eyed Suzie
Hey, pretty little black eyed Suzie
Hey, black eyed Suzie
Hey, Hey, Hey.

I'm walking drunk across the water
Some old man's gonna' lose his daughter.

Now some got drunk and some got boozy
I got drunk with Black Eyed Susie.

She'll Be Comin' Round the Mountain

Track 24

Key of G
G tuning – gDGBD

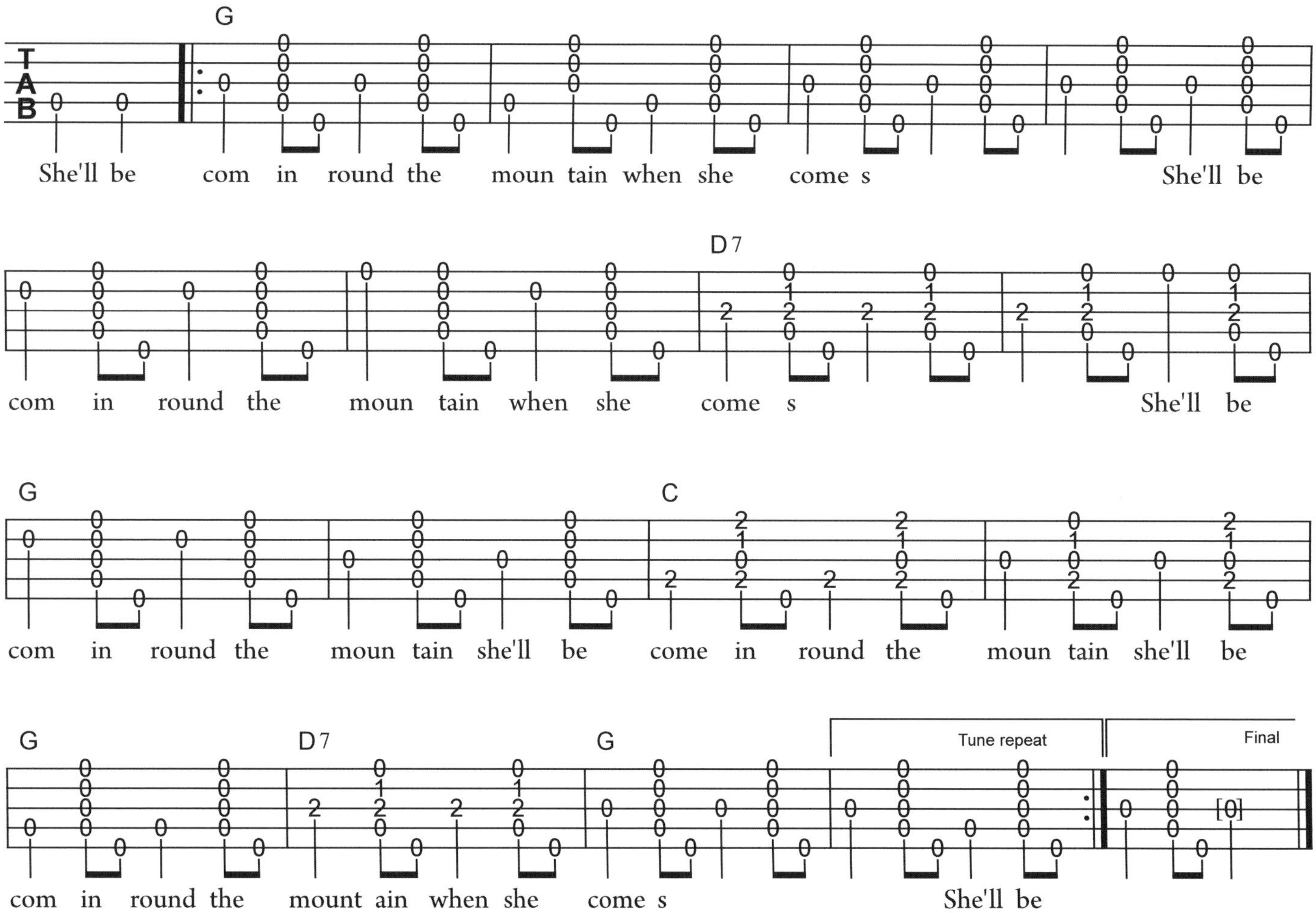

She'll be comin round the mountain when she comes
She'll be comin round the mountain when she comes
She'll be comin round the mountain, she'll be comin round the mountain
She'll be comin round the mountain when she comes

She'll be riding six white horses when she comes
She'll be riding six white horses when she comes
She'll be riding six white horses, She'll be riding six white horses
She'll be riding six white horses when she comes

We will all go down to meet her when she comes (x2)
We will all go down to meet her, we will all go down to meet her
We will all go down to meet her when she comes

We will kill the old red rooster when she comes...

Then we'll all have chicken and dumplins when she comes...

Well she'll have to sleep with grandma when she comes...

Mountain Dew

Track 25

Key of G
G tuning – gDGBD

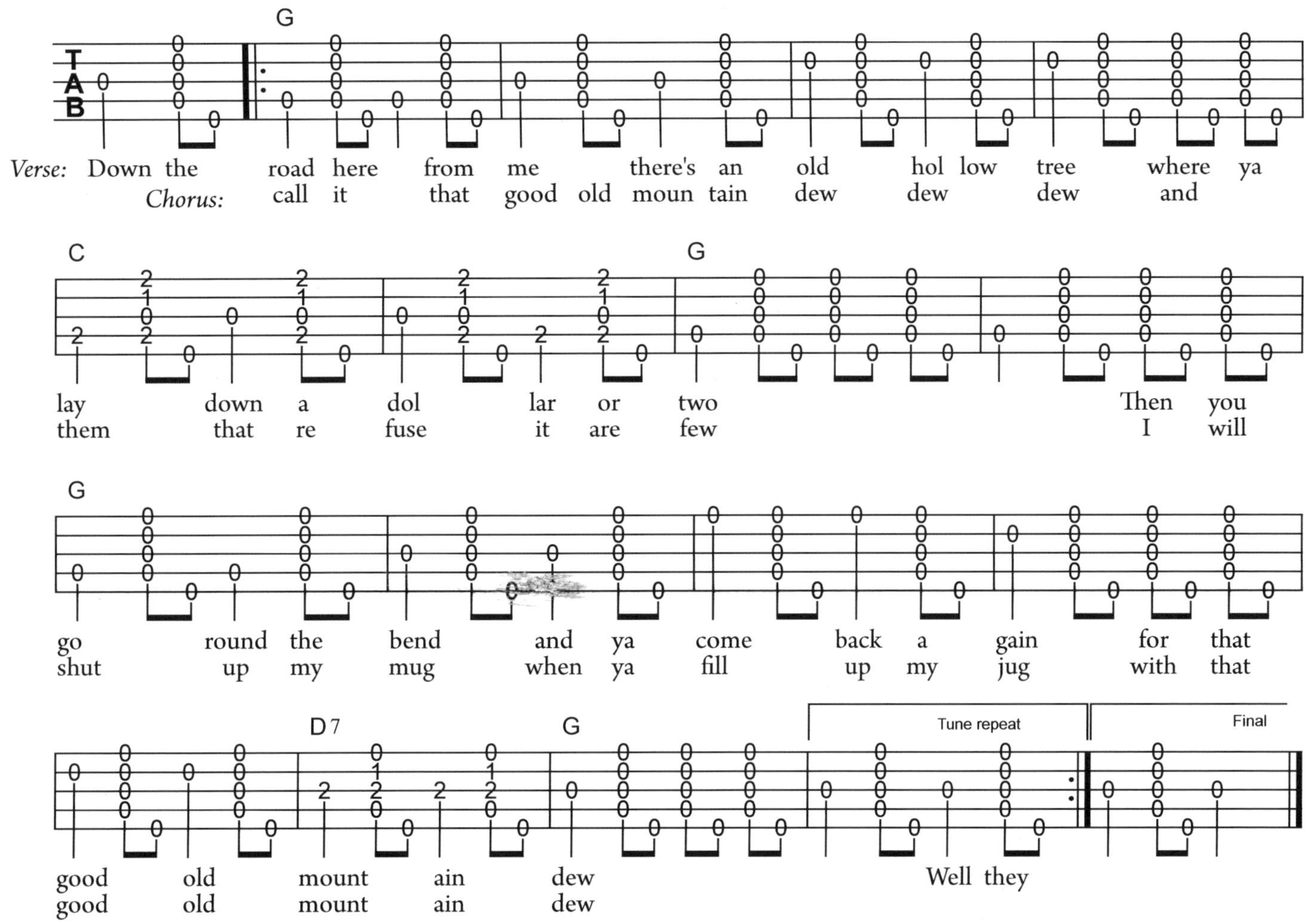

Verse:
Down the road here from me there's an old holler tree where ya lay down a dollar or two.
Then you go round the bend and ya come back again for that good ole mountain dew.

Chorus:
They call it that 'ol mountain dew and them that refuse it are few.
I'll shut up my mug when ya fill up my jug with some good ole mountain dew.

Now my uncle Nort, he's sawed off and short he measures about four foot two,
but he thinks he's a giant when you give him a pint of that good ole mountain dew.

Well the preacher rolled by with his head heisted high said his wife had been down with the flu,
and he thought that I ought just-a sell him a quart of that good ole mountain dew.

Well my brother Bill's got a still on the hill where he runs off a gallon or two.
Now the buzzards in the sky get so drunk they can't fly, from smellin' the good ole mountain dew.

The G Scale

Track 26

More single notes allows you to play more melody notes. To do that, all you really need is to learn the notes in the scale (remember do-re-me?) to choose from. Here is a G scale in tab.

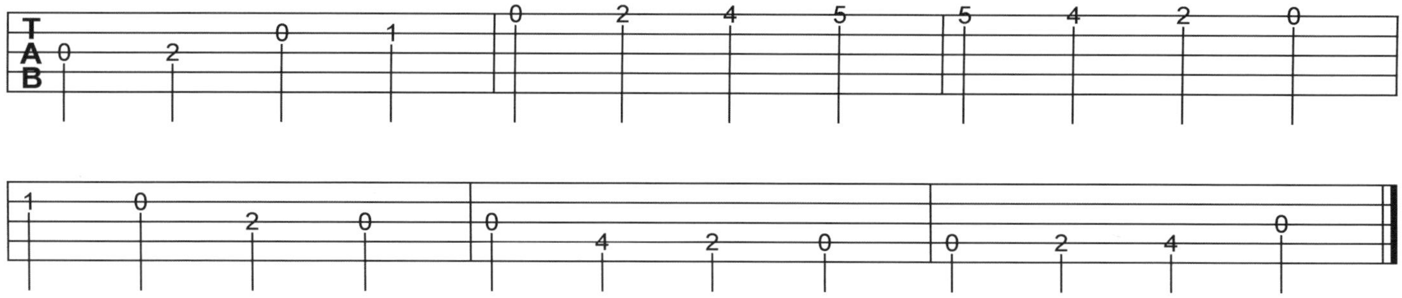

Example 11

Okay, let's put that to work with another song!

Free Little Bird

Track 27

Key of G
G tuning – gDGBD

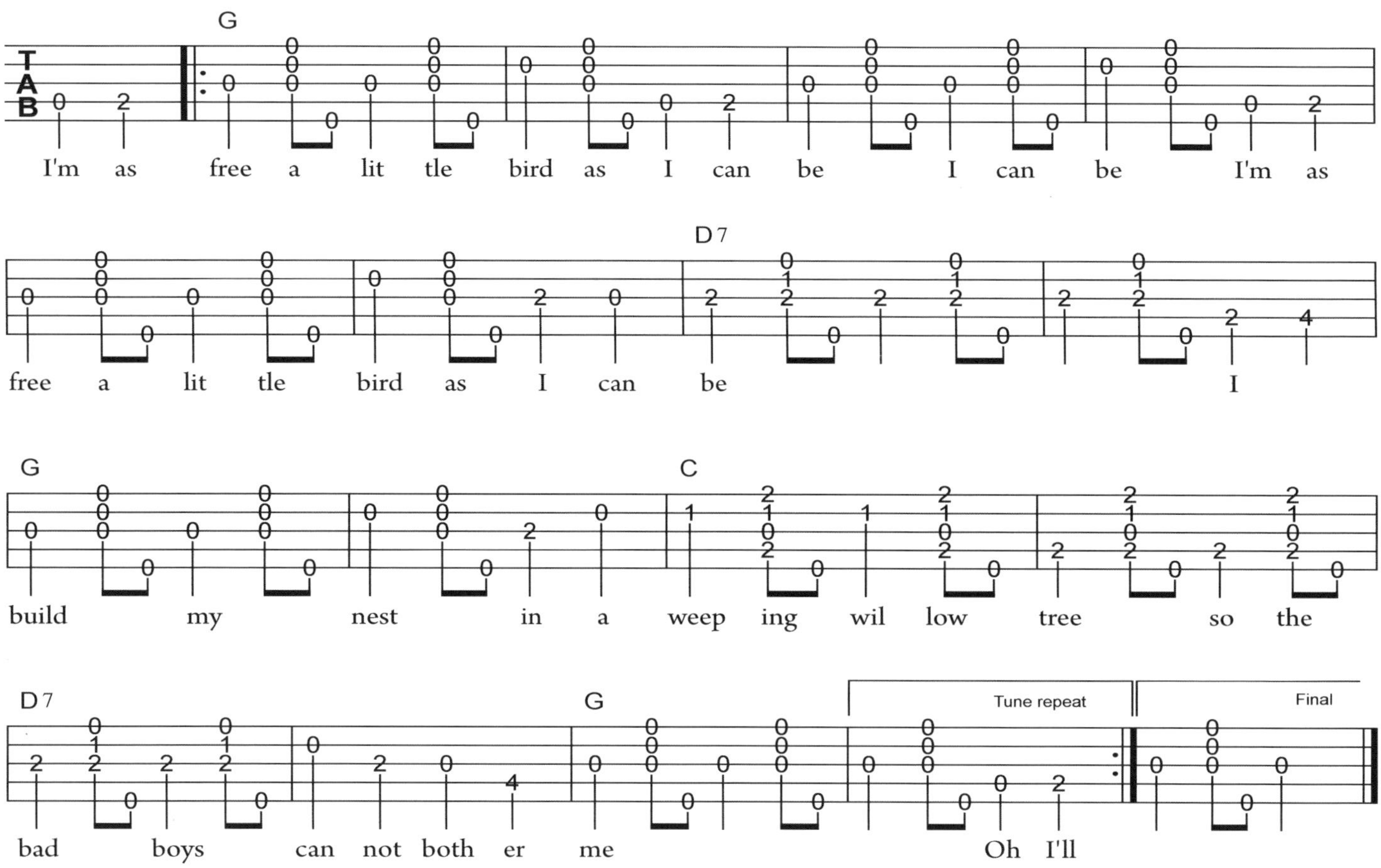

I'm as free a little bird as I can be, I can be; I'm as free a little bird as I can be
I build my house in the weeping willow tree, So the bad boys they cannot bother me.

Oh I'll never build my nest on the ground, on the ground; Oh I'll never build my nest on the ground
But I'll build my nest in a weeping willow tree, Where the bad boys cannot tear me down.

Oh I'll never steal honey from a tree, from a tree; I will never steal honey from a tree
But I'll steal me kiss from a sweet darlin's lips, And I'll carry her away across the sea.

Key of C – *One more chord*

Yes, with only one more chord, we get a whole other key! Why would you want another key? Well, lots of reasons, but I'll give you the most common one in folk music. Everyone sings and has a range of singing voice that fits best in one key over another. SO, while many folks can and do sing in G, some prefer other keys, often C. You will only need one more chord – an F – for that one.

I hear you, you are thinking, "Hey Dan, if we are getting a whole new key, how can we do it with just one more chord?" AH!!! Remember our I, IV, V system? In the key of G that meant if I was G, IV was C and our V (okay, V7) was D7. Now apply that here. If I is now C, count up to 4 – C, D, E, ***F*** – which makes our IV chord an F (our new chord). The V chord is – you got it – G! You already know C and G, so only one more chord is needed. The ***F*** chord. Oh, and by the way, you are now on the way to learning how the I-IV-V pattern helps you transpose or change any tune from one key to another, just by counting up and/or finding the I-IV-V of the key you are going to.

Fingering: I use my pinky at the 3rd fret of the 1st string, index finger at the first fret of the 2nd string, middle finger at the second fret of the 3rd string and my third finger at the third fret on the 4th string.

F Chord | F chord with basic stroke | F chord with basic rhythm - moving bass note

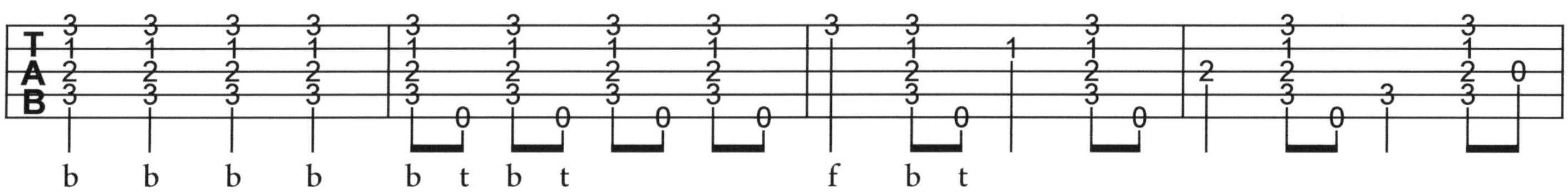

Key of C - I - IV - V - I pattern

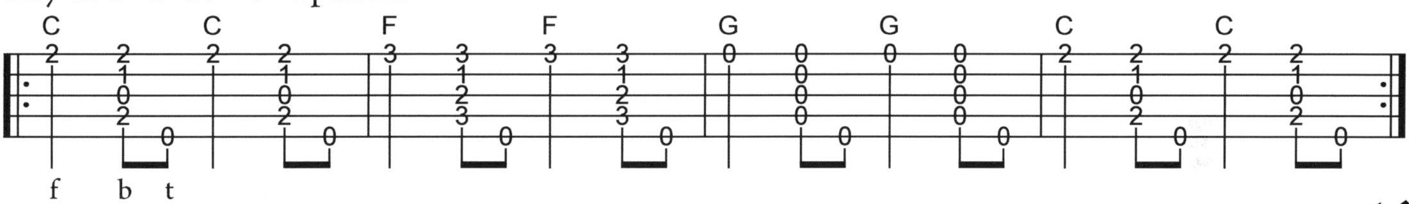

Key of C - Moving "bass" note - Song pattern

Track 28

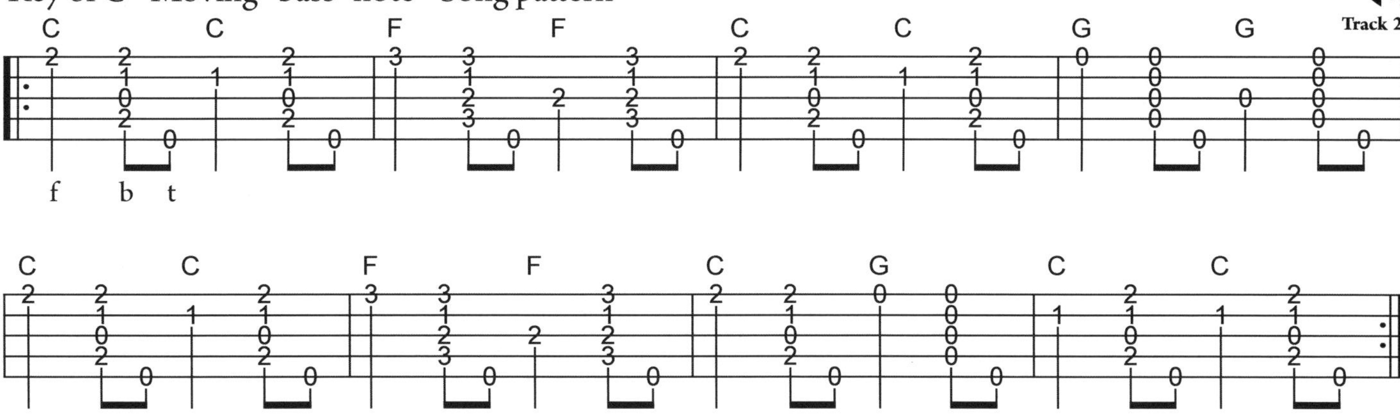

Example 12

Play the last part of this exercise until all of the changes are smooth.
Then play them in any order you like.

Froggy Went A'Courtin'

Track 29

Key of C
G tuning – gDGBD

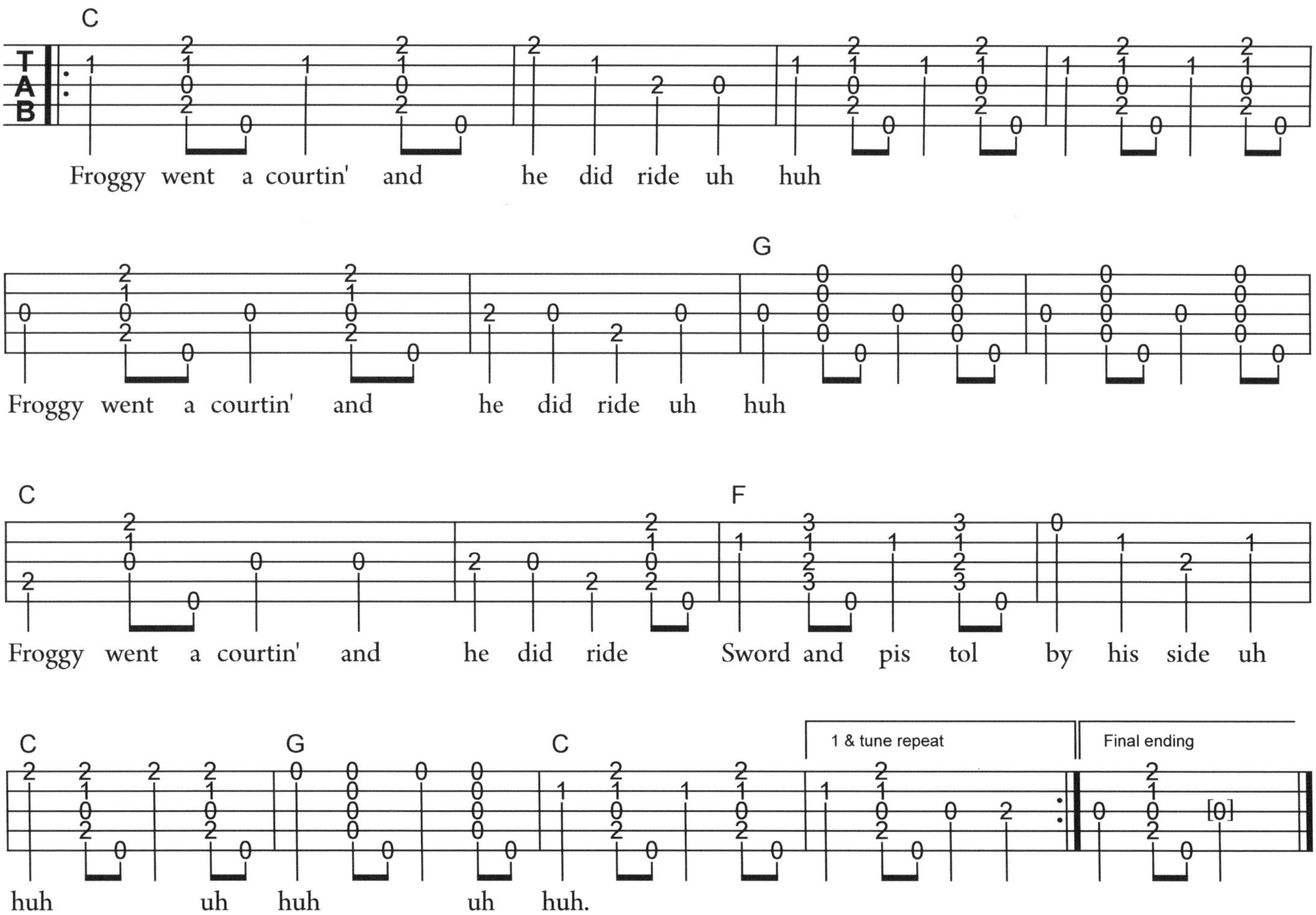

Froggy went a courtin' and he did ride uh-huh,
Froggy went a courtin' and he did ride uh-huh,
Froggy went a courtin' and he did ride,
Sword and pistol by his side,
uh-huh uh-huh, oh yeah.

He rode right up to Miss Mousie's door, uh-huh
He rode right up to Miss Mousie's door, uh-huh
He rode right up to Miss Mousie's door
Gave three loud raps, and a very big roar,
uh-huh uh-huh, oh yeah.

He said, "Miss Mouse, will you marry me? uh-huh
He said, "Miss Mouse, will you marry me? uh-huh
He said, "Miss Mouse, will you marry me?
And oh so happy we will be,
uh-huh uh-huh, oh yeah.

"Not without Uncle Rat's consent", uh-huh
"Not without Uncle Rat's consent", uh-huh
"Not without Uncle Rat's consent"
"Would I marry the President,"
uh-huh uh-huh, oh yeah.

Uncle Rat, he went downtown, uh-huh
Uncle Rat, he went downtown, uh-huh
Uncle Rat, he went downtown
To buy his niece a wedding gown,
uh-huh uh-huh, oh yeah.

Where shall the wedding supper be? uh-huh
Where shall the wedding supper be? uh-huh
Where shall the wedding supper be?
Way down yonder in the hollow tree,
uh-huh uh-huh, oh yeah.

Waltz Rhythm

Waltz rhythm is different from what we have been doing so far. Up until this point, all of the tunes have been in 4/4 time, which loosely means that there are four beats in each measure, (the top 4) and a quarter note receives one beat (the bottom 4). Waltz time is 3/4 time, which means that while a quarter note still receives one beat, there are now only three beats in each measure. Without getting into a long and boring discussion of music theory, lets just say that means instead of counting ONE two three four, ONE two three four, and emphasizing the first beat of each measure every fourth note, now it happens every three beats – ONE two three, ONE two three. Because of that, we change our rhythm from *bum diddy bum diddy* to *bum bum diddy* or *bum diddy diddy,* in order to provide a good basic back up rhythm with the right hand. With single notes to accentuate the melody we'll play *Oh My Darling Clementine* (yep, that one is a waltz) and *Down in the Valley*.

Oh My Darlin' Clementine

Track 30

Key of G
G tuning – gDGBD

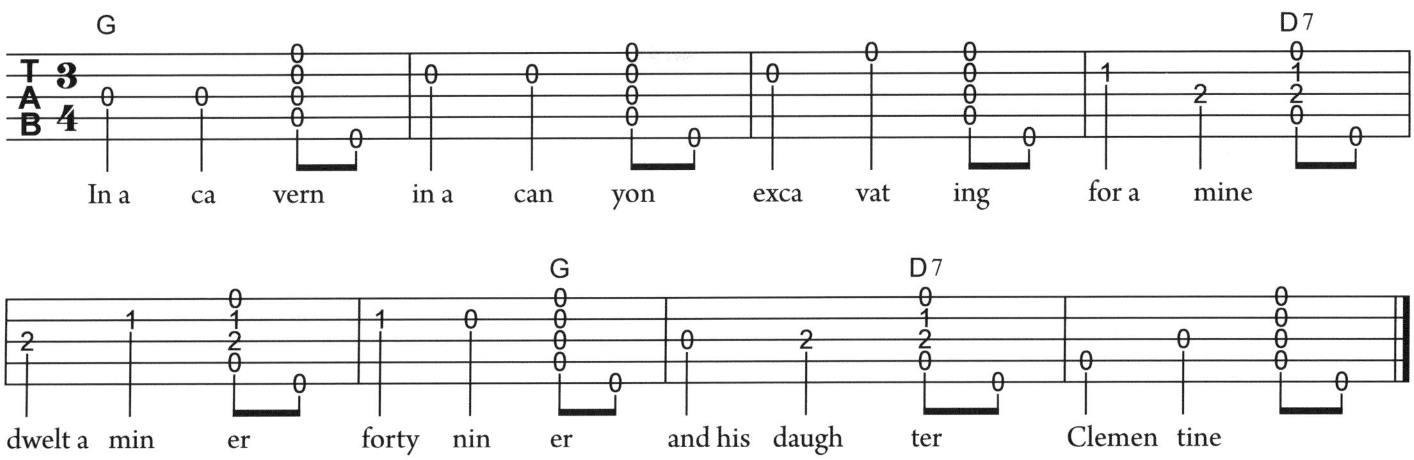

Verse:
In a Cavern, in a canyon
Excavating for a mine,
dwelt a miner forty-niner,
and his daughter Clementine.

Chorus:
Oh my Darling, Oh my Darling,
Oh my Darling Clementine.
Thou art lost and gone forever,
Dreadful sorry, Clementine.

Light she was and like a fairy,
And her shoes were number nine,
Herring boxes without topses
Sandals were for Clementine

In a churchyard on a hillside
Where the flowers grow and twine
There grow roses amongst the posies
Flowers for my Clementine.

Down in The Valley

Track 31

Key of G
G tuning – gDGBD

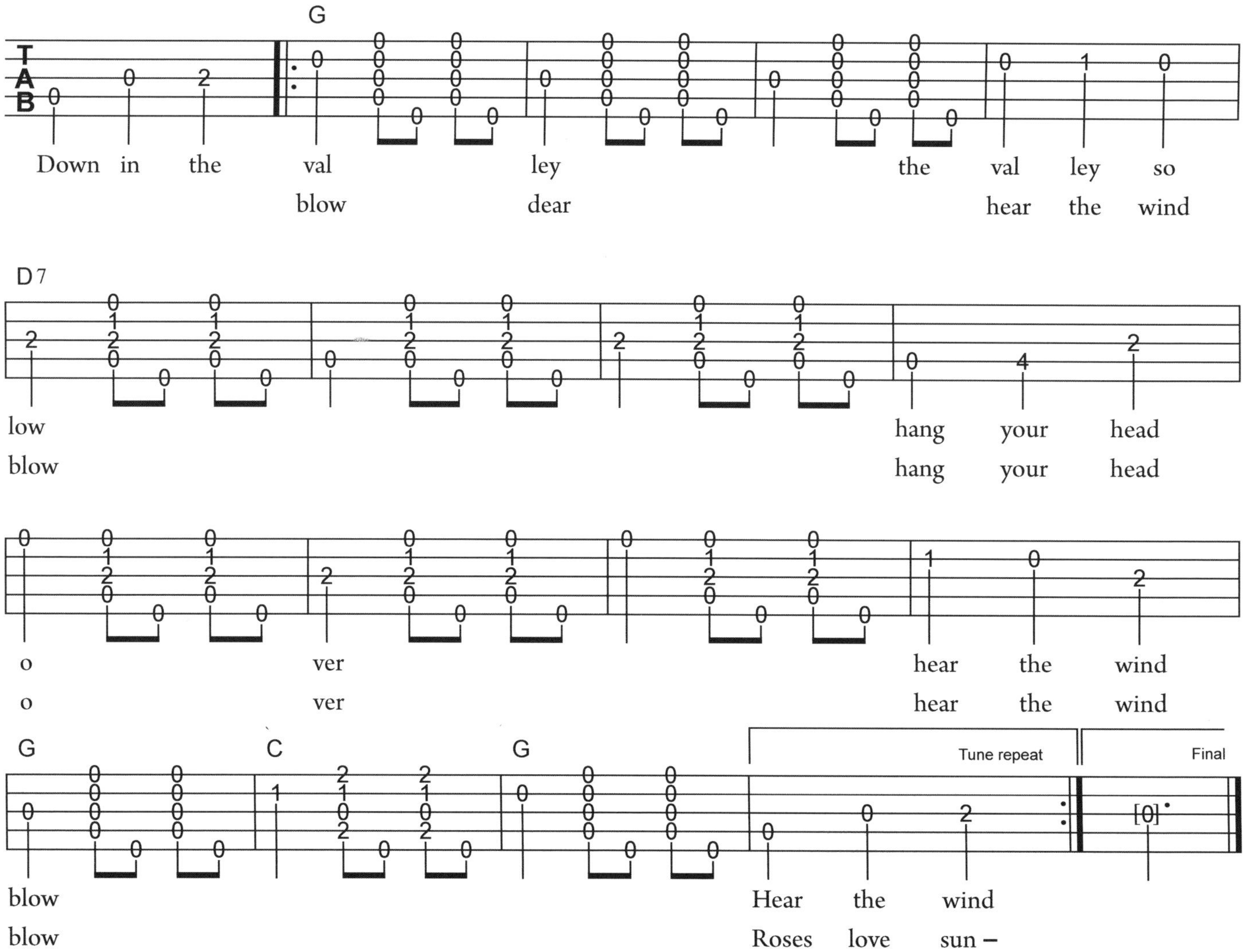

Down in the valley, the valley so low
Hang your head over, hear the wind blow
Hear the wind blow dear, hear the wind blow
Hang your head over, hear the wind blow

Build me a castle, forty feet high
So I can see her, as she rides by
As she rides by love, as she rides by
So I can see her, as she rides by

Roses love sunshine, violets love dew
Angels in heaven, know I love you
Know I love you dear, know I love you
Angels in heaven, know I love you.

Write me a letter, send it by mail
Send it in care of, the Birmingham Jail
Birmingham Jail love, Birmingham Jail
Send it in care of, the Birmingham Jail

5th string under *spike*

Homemade 5th string capo

The Capo and other keys

Capo – there was once an amusing booklet on clawhammer banjo playing that said, “a capo is that device that allows a banjo out of tune in one key to be instantly out of tune in any other key.” (Doc Stock Banjo Method). While that sounds funny on the face of it, it is not far from the truth. A capo is a mechanical finger or clamp that holds all of the melody strings (1st to 4th strings) down at the same time at the same fret, which then lets you change keys without having to retune your banjo.

There are a variety of good capos on the market, and I would hesitate to tell you which one to get. Most of them (Schubb, Kyser, Paige and G7 to name only a few) are very easy to use, protect the instrument and give even and accurate pressure for around $25. However, I would warn you against using the cheap elastic ones because they are cumbersome, not very accurate, and the rivets in the strap tend to severely scratch the banjo’s neck.

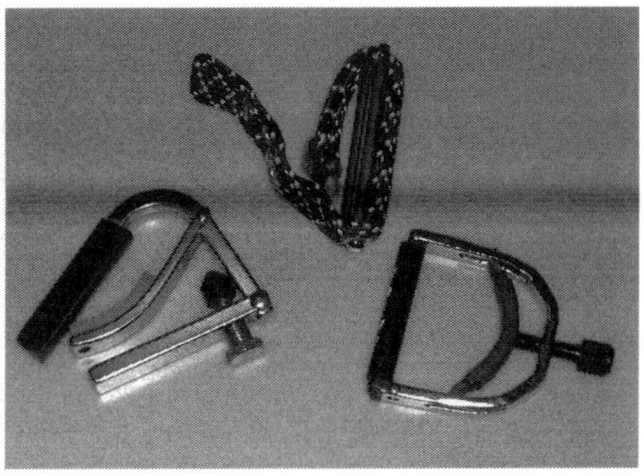

To use the capo, you put it on the neck just behind or on the headstock side of the fret you want to capo. There are several different designs of capos, so you will have to check the instructions that came with yours to see how it works (spring clamp, screw setting, and etc.) but they all do the same thing even if they do it in different ways. This changes the key of your banjo in half steps according to the fret you are capoed at.

Each fret is a half step, so if your four open strings are tuned for G tuning (4-1 DGBD) and you put the capo at the first fret, you bring the banjo up to G# - or one half step. Go to the second fret and you are now in A. Your capoed strings are now EAC#E (4th to 1st strings) and you are now ALMOST in the key of A. Why almost? Because you still have to deal with the fifth (short) string.

While the main capo clamps on the first four strings, you still need to retune the 5th string up the same number of half steps (each fret = 1/2 step up the musical scale) as you did for the capo. There are a variety of ways to do this, and the easiest is to just retune the fifth string to match the NEW fifth fret on the first string. SO, if you capoed up 2 frets to the key of A, then you would retune the fifth string to “a” also. BUT this only works up to a point. Above that “a”, the string will most likely break, so we need another alternative if you want to capo more than two frets up from the key of G.

You will need a 5th string capo (see photo), which works much like the capo described above, except that it only hit the 5th string and is permanently installed on the banjo, or *spikes* – actually small HO railroad spikes which allow you to slip the 5th string under them acting like a capo (see photo page 32). Both of these items should be installed for you by a competent luthier familiar with banjo spikes and fifth string capos. Or, you can make a quick and handy one from a stick pen cap like in the photo also on page 32!

Permanently mounted 5th string capo

Once you are all tuned up, the notes of your strings will now be tuned aEAC#E, which puts you in the key of A. Your old 2nd fret is now your new nut, so you have to count up to the new 5th fret, NOT counting the one where the capo is (ie. the seventh fret without the capo becomes the new fifth fret). SO, the tab numbers refer to the fret number after the one the where capo is placed.

The finger positions of your I, IV, and V chords when you are capoed up are exactly the same. Only the names changed one full musical step up, so the G is now A, C is D and D is E. Oh, you can also play in the key of D by using the F (which is now G). I-IV-V starts to make sense, eh? You can change to other keys too by simply moving the capo, adjusting the 5th string and using the same I–IV–V positions.

PHEW!!!! That was too much like work wasn't it? SO, lets relax with a new tune.

Old Joe Clark—I

Track 32

Key of A
(G tuning - gDGBD - capo 2)

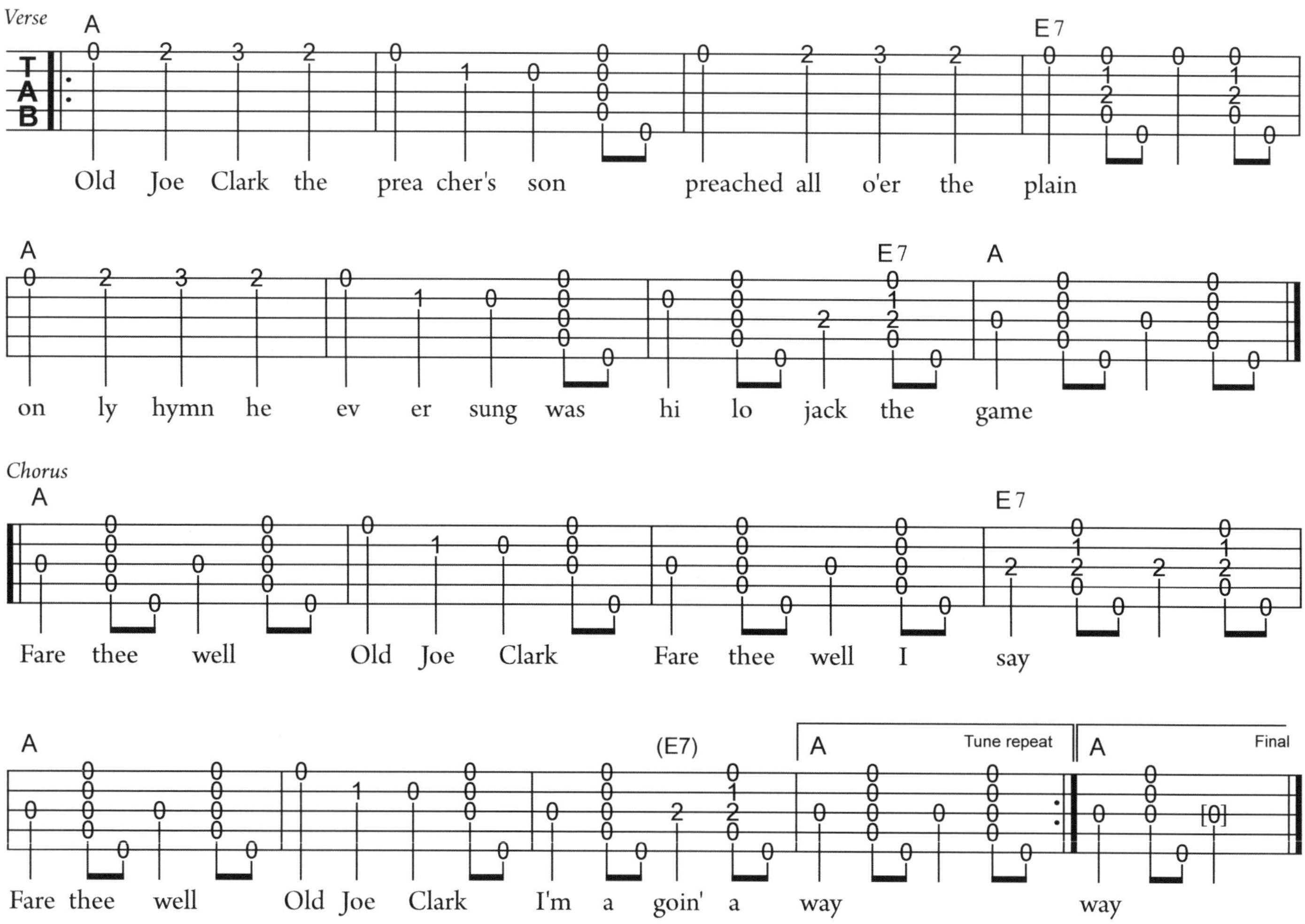

There are many versions of this song, so here are a couple of verses to get you started.

Old Joe Clark the preacher's son; preached all over the plain
Only hymn he ever sung was hi/lo jack and the game

Chorus:
Fare thee well Old Joe Clark; Fare thee well I say;
Fare thee well Old Joe Clark; I'm a goin' away.

Old Joe Clark had a house fifteen stories high
And every room in that thar house was filled with chicken pie

The VII Chord

The *VII* chord refers to this being the 7th chord of the key, so since we are in A, the VII chord is a G (A-B-C-D-E-F-G). (If we were in G, the VII chord would be an F). In the key of A, the VII chord is a G. You actually already know this chord. It was your old friend, the F chord, which we used in the G tuning to allow us to play in the key of C. (See page 29 if you need to review the chord's tab figure).

The VII (7) chord can make a normal plain tune sound more exotic. It doesn't appear often, but enough that I wanted to give you one tune this way. And it will be one we already know – *Old Joe Clark.* This time we are going to play it with a VII chord in the second part. Many folks play it this way.

Old Joe Clark—II
with VII chord

Track 33

Key of A
(G tuning - gDGBD - capo 2)

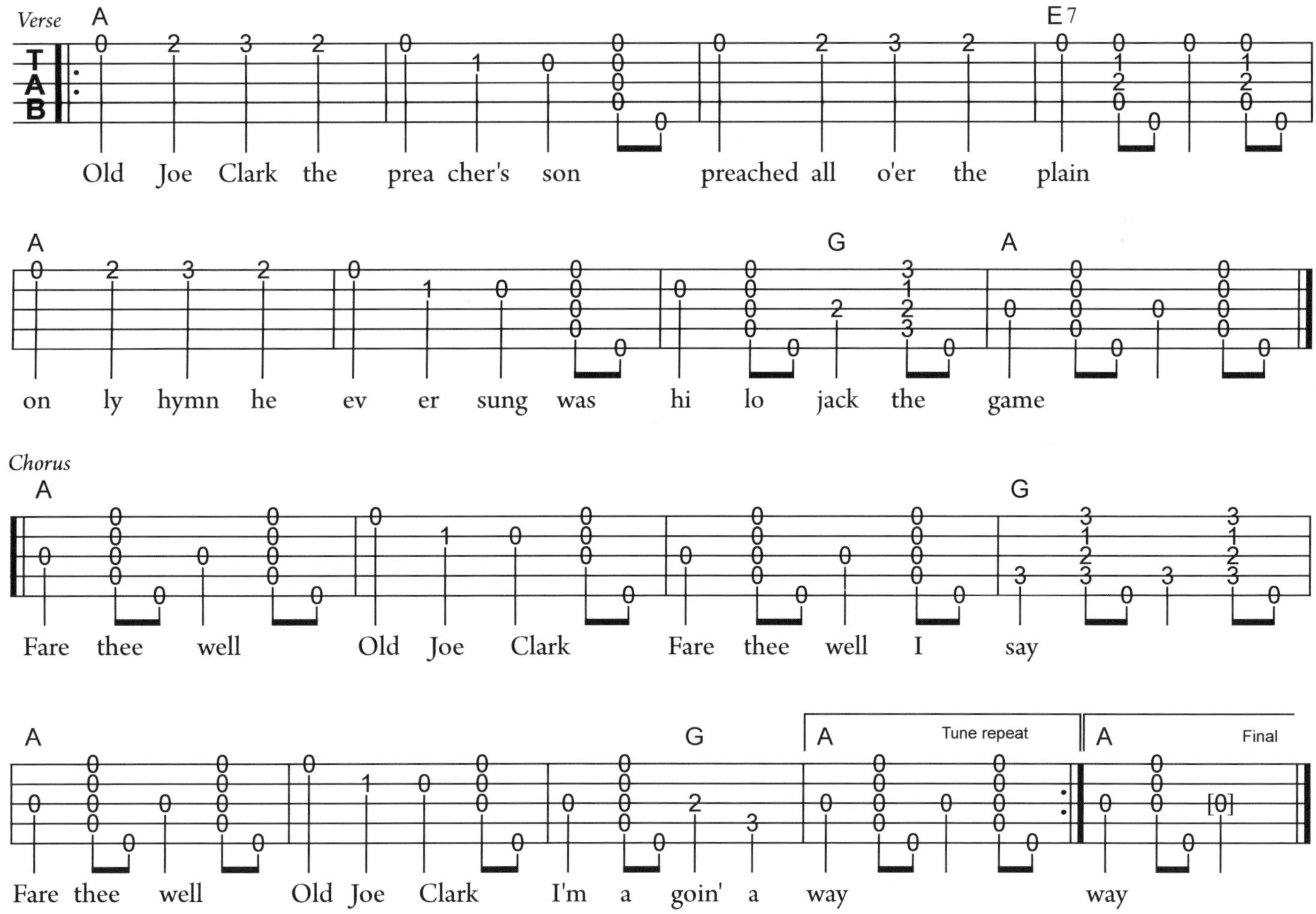

WOW, you have really worked hard! I do know you are making great progress and having fun too.

There is only one more technique to present to you, and that is *Hammer–ons, Pull–offs and Slides.* Yeah, looks like three but we group them together because they accomplish much the same thing. They all give you different ways to play more notes, particularly on the second half of any beat. This is the last technique that I am going to cover in this book, so let's get going!

Hammer–ons, pull–offs and slides

Up until now, the only place you have played the second half of a beat is after the strum and with the thumb, and *that* was always an open 5th string. These next techniques give you a nice introduction into more advanced tune playing and are what Miss Jennifer often calls the important "bells and whistles" that make banjo playing so dynamic. It also lets you get a few more notes in when playing a tune!

Hammer–On – A *hammer–on* occurs when you place a left hand finger down on a string hard enough to hear the note sound. It can be to a fret from an open string or another fret "up" the scale from an already fretted string. Here are three hammer–ons tabbed out for you in example 13.

Track 34

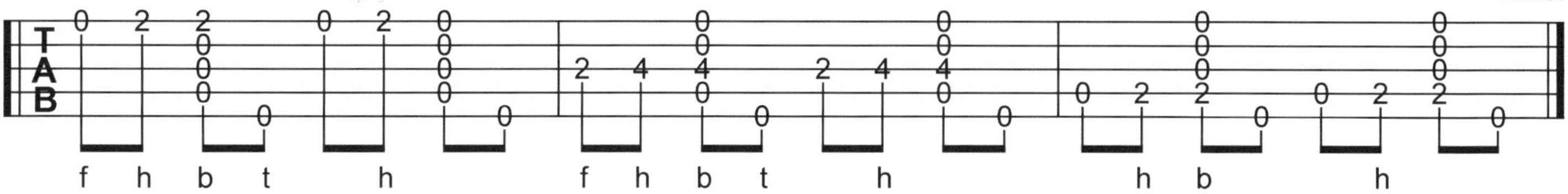

Example 13

(Note: I put all of the right and left hand notations under the first measure to start, then gradually reduce the notations to only the ones you should "need").

Pull–Off – a *pull–off* is sometimes called "left hand pizzicatto" and involves plucking a string with a ***left*** hand finger as you *pull–off* of one note to a fret below, or another note lower on the scale. Here are three different pull–offs in tab in example 14.

Track 35

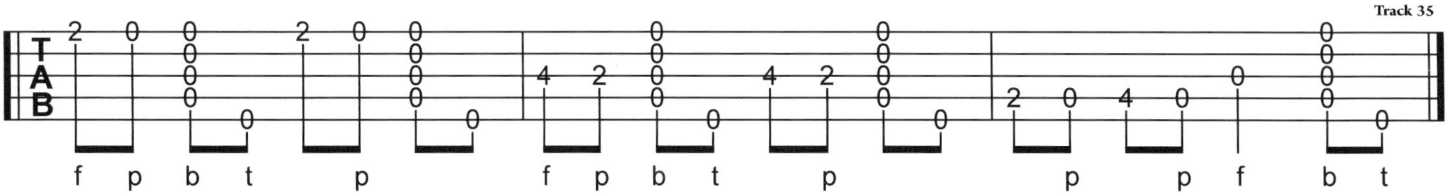

Example 14

Slide – A *slide* occurs when you move your finger from one fretted note to another fret, up OR down the scale without fully lifting it off of the fingerboard as you *slide* from one note to the other. Notice the curved line above the notes of the slide. That is called a *slur.* Some folks also put a slur over hammers and pulls, but I only put them on slides because they indicate a continuous tone from start to finish of the slide, whereas hammer–ons and pull–offs are each made up of two seperate notes or tones. Here are three types of the slides written out for you in example 15.

Track 36

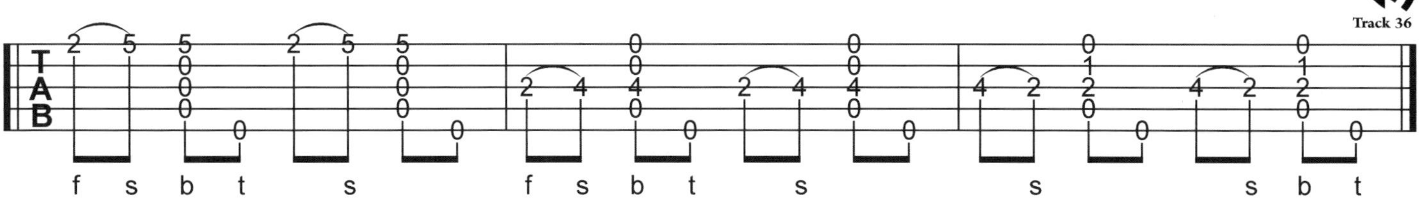

Example 15

Let's use them all in one final tune. We'll combine this with all of the other techniques you have learned in this book to give us a full blown version of a song you played early in this book, *Cripple Creek.* As a closing piece at this point in your study, this version should be a challange as it adds new techniques AND uses all of your combined skills. It might not seem easy at first, but you have worked hard to acquire what you need to make this song, well, sing! Back to G tuning and the key of G.

Cripple Creek—II

Track 37

Key of G
G tuning – gDGBD

with Hammer–ons, Pull–offs and Slides
or as Miss Jennifer says, "All the bells and whistles!"

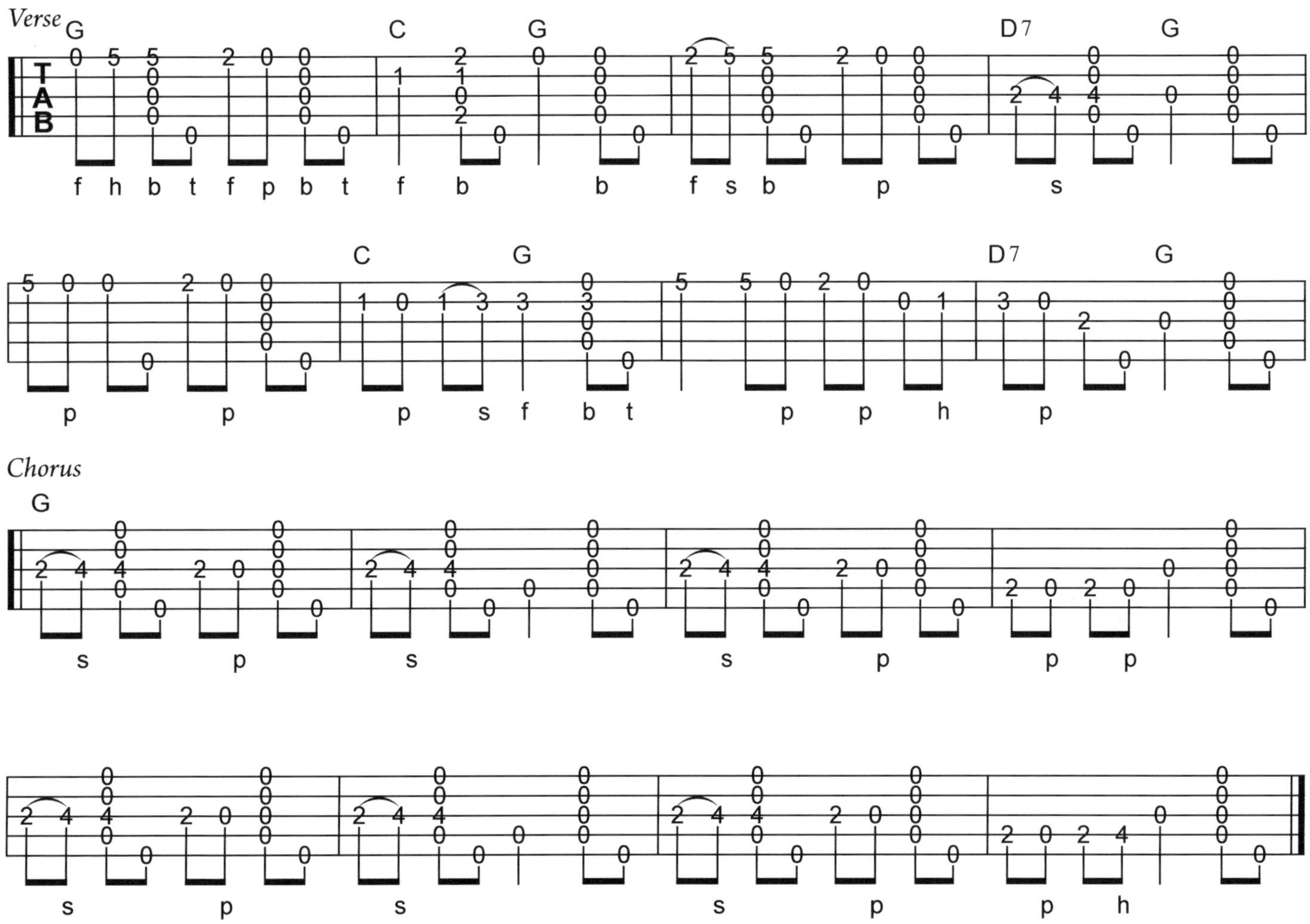

Since we did this one before, you will find the words back on page 21.

Give yourselves a big hand! You've done it!

Thanks for taking this time with me. I do hope you have enjoyed this journey through your *First Lessons – Folk Banjo*. I look forward to working further with you as you continue your journey. Remember, listen to lots of music – espically the folk masters that have come before you, work to be the best you can be, sing and play with others and most importantly:

Play Nice!

Dan "Clawdan" Levenson

Other products by Dan Levenson

Wade Ward - Clawhammer Master - Banjo tablature with companion audio (MB22243M) Tunes of clawhammer master Wade Ward co-written with Bob Carlin. Two tabs of each of 28 tunes both as the master played them and as they are often interpreted today.

Kyle Creed - Clawhammer Master - Banjo tablature with companion audio (MB22137M) Tunes of clawhammer master Wade Ward co-written with Bob Carlin. Two tabs of each of 28 tunes both as the master played them and as they are often interpreted today.

Old Time Festival Tunes for Fiddle & Mandolin - Tablature with Standard Notation and audio - Mel Bay Publications (MB20313M) 117 Old Time favorites with basic and advanced standard notation plus a tab line for mandolin and fiddle.

Gospel Tunes for Clawhammer Banjo - Tablature with Standard Notation and companion audio - Mel Bay Publications (MB21432M) - 27 Favorite Gospel tunes and hymns in an easy to play format.

Old Time Festival Tunes for Clawhammer Banjo - Tablature with Standard Notation and audio - Mel Bay Publications (MB20313M) 117 Old Time favorites with basic and advanced tab plus a standard notation line for other instruments.

Clawhammer Banjo From Scratch - Mel Bay Publications (MB20190M) - This book starts at the beginning. 12 common jam session tunes are presented in double thumb and drop thumb technique in Double D tuning. Includes audio.

Clawhammer Banjo From Scratch - DVD set - Mel Bay Publications -(MB 5003 DVD) - Clawhammer banjo players, start here! This instructional video teaches the basics "From Scratch" through the double thumb Spotted Pony in double C. Disc 2 Tunes you up to Double D and then picks up and adds drop thumb, hammer-ons, pull-offs, more.

Buzzard Banjo Clawhammer Style - Mel Bay Publications (MB99126M) - Tab book with companion audio. 25 tunes tabbed out as played by Dan Levenson with companion audio of the tabs. Includes some basic instruction.

Traveling Home (Buzzard 2005 CD) - Banjo, fiddle, guitar and song solos and duos with Dan, Miss Jennifer and Rick Barron. Tunes: *Red Haired Boy; Leaving Home; John Brown's Dream; Dry & Dusty; Camp Chase/Jenny Git Around; Texas Gals; John Lover's Gone; Texas; Milwaukee Blues; Kentucky John Henry; Lost Indian; Boatman; Durang's Hornpipe; Monkey on a Dogcart; Whistling Rufus; Sandy Boys; Arkansas Traveler/Mississippi Sawyer/Rock the Cradle Joe; Banjo Tramp.*

Barenaked Banjos (Buzzard 2002 CD) - 24 all solo banjo pieces. 4 different banjos! Tunes: *Katy Hill; Logan County Blues; Little Billie Wilson; Dr. Dr.; Texas Gals; Forked Deer; Staten Island; Liza Poor Gal; Johnny Don't Get Drunk; Rocky Pallet; Needlecase; Old Bell Cow; Fortune; Old Molly Hare/Rag Time Annie; Soldier's Joy; Billy in the Low Ground; Joke on the Puppy; Breaking Up Christmas; Whiskey Before Breakfast; Hangman's Reel; Duck River; Flying Indian; June Apple; Wild Horses at Stoney Point.*

Light of the Moon (Buzzard 2001 CD) - Fiddle tunes to folk songs are what you will find in this recording. Dan is joined on a few songs with other musicians including Annie Trimble of the Boiled Buzzards, and his son Jonathan. Tunes: *June Apple; Cindy; Rushing the Pepper; Climbing the Golden Stairs; All God's Critters; Jaybird/Moses Hoe the Corn; Old Rip; The Fox; Rockin' Jenny; Soppin' the Gravy; Willow Waltz; Darlin' Corey; Buffalo Gals; Yellow Rose of Texas; Shelvin' Rock/Old Mother Flanagan; Snake River Reel; Hard Traveling; John Stenson's #2; Roseville Fair; Front Porch Waltz.*

New Frontier (Blue rose 1001 CD) - All instrumentals w/Dan Levenson on banjo, fiddle and guitar and Kim Murley on hammered dulcimer and Yang Qin (Chinese hammered dulcimer). Tunes: *Kitchen Girl/Growling Old Man, Grumbling Old Woman; Weaving Girl; Lullaby; Pachinko; Liza Poor Gal/ Traveling Down the Road; Dance of the Yao People; Red Haired Boy; Duke of Kent's Waltz; Thunder on a Dry Day; Horse Race; Flying Indian; Dragon Boat; Mackinac Bats; Rosy Cloud Follows the Moon; Song of the Frontier; Cherry Blossom Waltz.*

Early Bird Special (Buzzard 1004 CD) - Dan plays with The Boiled Buzzards Old Time Stringband. Tunes: *Smith's Reel; Beasties in the Sugar; Wooden Nickel; Brandywine/Three Forks of Reedy; The Engineers Don't Wave From the Train Anymore; Black Widow Romp; Young Guns and Miners; Boys Them Buzzards Are Flying; Lulu Loves Them Young; Bitter Creek; Lost Everything; Nixon's Farewell; Teabag Blues; Sadie at the Back Door/Waiting for Nancy; You Can't Get There From Here; Snake River Reel; Grey Haired Dancing Girl; Cliff's Waltz.* Mostly instrumental (vocals on 2 cuts) banjo, fiddle, guitar, and acoustic bass.

Eat at Joe's (Buzzard 1003 CD) - Dan plays with the Boiled Buzzards. Tunes: *Paddy on the Turnpike; John Brown's March/Waiting for the Federals; Snake River Reel; Hollow Poplar; Spotted Pony; Dinah/Wake Up Susan; Black Widow Romp; Katy Hill; Nixon's Farewell; Shady Grove; Spring in the Valley; Cuffy; The Year of Jubilo/Yellow Rose of Texas; Jimmy in the Swamp; Nixon's Farewell (w/double fiddles); Julianne Johnson; Tombigbee Waltz.* All instrumental music played on banjo, fiddle, guitar, and acoustic bass.

Fine Dining (Buzzard 1002 CD) - Dan plays with the Boiled Buzzards. Tunes: *Shuffle About; Little Dutch Girl; John Brown's Dream; Liza Jane; Goodbye Miss Liza; Booth Shot Lincoln; Briarpicker Brown; Monkey on a Dogcart; Fortune; Shenandoah Falls; Three Ponies; Jaybird; Forked Deer/Doctor Doctor; Leaving Home; Rock the Cradle Joe; Old Mother Flanagan; Santa Claus; Too Young to Marry; Roscoe; Stambaugh Waltz.* Mostly instrumental (vocals on 2 cuts) banjo, harmonica, guitar, and acoustic bass.

Salt and Grease (Buzzard 1001 CD) - is The Boiled Buzzards' first album. Tunes: *Julianne Johnson; 3 Thin Dimes; Durang's Hornpipe; Milwaukee Blues; Muddy Roads; Log Chain/Railroading Across the Rocky Mountains (Marmaduke's Hornpipe); Billy in the Lowground; Yellow Barber; Little Billy Wilson; Sandy Boys; Southtown; Rochester Schottische; Kansas City Reel; June Apple; Bull at the Wagon; Sally Ann Johnson; Nail That Catfish to a Tree; Icy Mountain; Benton's Dream; Sadie's Waltz.* Mostly instrumental (vocals on 2 cuts) banjo, harmonica, guitar, and acoustic bass.

For more information and to order Dan's products, please go to www.Clawdan.com

Dan Levenson is a Southern Appalachian native who has grown up with the music of that region. Today he is considered a respected master teacher and performer of both the Clawhammer banjo & Appalachian style fiddle.

Dan has won awards on both instruments including first place at the 2005 Ohio Clawhammer Banjo Championship and Grand Champion at the 2010 Ajo, AZ fiddle contest. He has over 10 recordings both with his band The Boiled Buzzards and as a solo artist.

Dan performs and teaches regularly throughout the country. He has taught at many of the traditional music schools and camps including the John C. Campbell Folk School, Mars Hill, Maryland Banjo Academy, The Ozark Folk Center at Mountain View, AR and Banjo Camp North. He currently also runs various clawhammer banjo, fiddle and stringband workshops as well as his innovative *Clawcamp* throughout the year.

Dan is the Mel Bay author of *Clawhammer Banjo From Scratch, Buzzard Banjo Clawhammer Style, Old Time Festival Tunes for Clawhammer Banjo, Old Time Festival Tunes for Fiddle & Mandolin, Gospel Tunes for Clawhammer Banjo, Kyle Creed Clawhammer Banjo Master* and *Wade Ward Clawhammer Banjo Master*. He writes for *The Old Time Herald* and is a writer and editor for *Banjo Newsletter's Old Time Way*.

For Dan's books, recordings and more information about Dan please go to www.Clawdan.com